GW00863282

A Year with Nell

A dog and person diary

By

and

Barbara Elliott

For, in no particular order, Ruth Dickie, Val Green and Helen Robinson – friends and readers (on my mailing list) of my scribbles.

My son and daughter, Ben and Hannah, for laughing in all the right places!

Nell at 15 months

I have had dogs before; four to be precise. Having said goodbye to the fourth, I waited for some time before thinking that I could welcome another. I chose a Labrador for somewhat selfish reasons; I wanted a short haired dog that would be easy to keep clean and dry in Devon's wet winters and because they are good family dogs. I considered rehoming a rescue dog – a noble gesture – but with three young grandchildren I wanted to train a puppy with them – it works both ways! Then Nell came into my life with a mind, an attitude and a diary all her own …

May 2022

Nell: We're told that a prospective new owner is coming to 'view' us. I look suitably cute and hard done by as I'm the smallest of the litter. My brothers are rough playing when the visitors come.

There are four visitors. Two are very small.

I'm chosen! (That looking cute must have worked.) She'll call me Nell. I also heard this – she thought of calling me Bess but two local dogs are called Ben and Benson – too many B's!

Me: She looks so small. I know that one is supposed to take the liveliest and most inquisitive puppy but I've never been drawn to flashy - either dogs or people!

My daughter and her two girls also agree with the choice. Nell is identified with a red collar.

Am I ready?

June 2022

Nell: She came alone today. She gave me a cuddle and I snuggled into her. Cosy. I stayed still. She did a lot of talking with the family who bred me. She's been away on holiday. Will she take me away today?

Me: She's grown. I leave an old cardigan (minus the buttons!) for her to have something of mine.

Now I've to get everything ready; puppy carrier, all the shoes moved. She'll sleep in the boot room so all chewable items need to be moved elsewhere. I'm getting a cardboard box for her bed. This sounds cheap – well, no cost at all! – and I know she'll chew it but it will be snug so that she feels safe.

Nell: I've been told to be on my best behaviour! I'm leaving today! A new home! I hope there's lots of food and no other dogs to fight for it.

She'd made me a cosy bed that I could curl up in and it had my blanket in it. She gave me food and there was only me to eat it. She watched me eating and seemed pleased that I ate it all!

She has a little door that I can use to go outside. I push it with my nose and off I go. Fun!

She shut me outside **all night**!

Me: The carrier won't fit in my car so I'm given a lift in a car that can house it.

The breeder and I fill out all the paperwork and I'm given a goody bag and two bags of the food Nell's been having.

I know that I've to be tough to begin with, firm.

I show her the dog flap and put down puppy training pads. She likes the cardboard box and doesn't need any encouragement to eat her food!

All night! All night! She whined and cried. I was determined not to go down to her. My neighbours have a holiday let and have warned their guests that a tiny puppy had arrived. Good job they all have double glazing!

At six o'clock, I felt that I had to go down and see what damage had been incurred as she sounded as if she was outside. This is my fault! I'd shown Nell how to go out through the dog flap but not that she could get back in! No wonder she was so upset!

The good news is that she was pleased to see me.

Nell: In my bed I have my blanket and a teddy which came in my goody bag. I snuggle with them but I also have some other toys.

She clears up after me and takes me into a garden.

Today we have visitors – the little girls, her daughter and a big dog called Sophie. Sophie looks like me but much, much bigger. She's like my mum. I can tell she likes me and I know to be passive – I roll over onto my back. We play together inside and outside. I follow her around.

The little girls play with me and teach me how to get back into my room; one calls from outside and then the other calls from inside and I go back and forth through the dog flap. I'm tired.

Me: I'm so pleased that Sophie and Nell get on so well. Sophie was trying to teach Nell how to play tug of war. Nell didn't get it!

Outside, Sophie taught Nell a less welcome game – how to go into all the barns and find cat poo to eat. Ugh! I don't have cats but there are four nearby.

Is this revolting poo eating habit a Labrador thing? I hope Sophie doesn't teach Nell how to roll in fox poo which is another of her skills!

Nell was shattered after the visit. I had a quiet evening!

Nell: Another visit! This time it was Sandra – a human – and Benson, a big dog! We went into the garden. Benson seems to like me. I was subservient towards him and to Sandra. Sandra gave me a little biscuit. I like Sandra.

Me: It's good for Nell to get on with Benson. I expect that they'll walk together when Nell's older.

I'm trying to house train Nell. She seems to have learned that poo's can be done outside but she pee's anywhere and everywhere! I keep using anti-bacterial spray. Occasionally, she uses the puppy training mats at night.

Nell: When she says "Nell! Come!" I go to her and she praises me. Well, I would go to her – she feeds me! Sometimes, she throws a toy. Why? Is she annoyed with it?

Me: She knows her name and comes when I call her – every time! Hurrah! However, the constant cleaning up of puddles in the house is wearing. I put her through the dog flap and mop up but I'm sure I show my annoyance; I sometimes shout 'NO!' I think she maybe has too much space during the day since she seems to go outside to pee at night. During the day, she has the boot room, the hall and the kitchen/diner. She doesn't seem to mind in which of these she leaves puddles. However, the hall appears to be the favourite!

Nell: She's taken me outside (out of the gate) to pee lots of times today and is muttering something about the car.

Oh! She put me in a carrier thing. Zipped in with one of my toys, off we go in the car. It is very hot and we have a window open a bit. I'm quiet. Where am I going? Is she taking me back? Doesn't she like me enough to keep me? I have to make a little cry sound. She carried me into a place with a waiting room. She calls it 'The Vet's'.

I am taken out and put on a high table by a nice lady. There's talking - about me. I think the lady likes me and she puts something on the table for me to lick up! Delicious! She combs me. Why? My hair is really short. I saw my sister!!

Me: Nell was quiet in the car and very good waiting in the carrier to go into the examination room. I wonder what she's thinking?

I ask about the peeing on the hall tiles, wondering if the urine smell lingers in the grouting. The vet suggests I use biological soap powder to wash them with as the enzymes get rid of the attractive (to Nell) smell. Who knew?

Another vet came in to see Nell. She has Nell's sister, Dora. I saw Dora, too. Nell didn't feel her vaccination – too busy licking up the paste spread on the table!

The vet checked her for 'walking dandruff' (!) as I said she'd been scratching. All seems clear.

Nell's last vaccination will be in two weeks' time. I have a flea/louse – but not tick – treatment to give administer in a few days.

Nell: **I am really ill.** . . I've brought up at least five days' worth of food and have to go to the loo <u>all the time!</u>

She hasn't told me off even though she's had to wash my blanket and teddy and clear up all the mess.

I am very tired.

She gave me some lovely food.

Me: I've heard of projectile vomiting but projectile pooing? I saw her lift her tail and the liquid shot out about eighteen inches! Poor Nell. She's feeling very sorry for herself and is sleeping - then dashing outside.

Here's the problem: Nell tries everything by mouth! Every plant, stone, twig, snail shell. She's been chewing all sorts of wood. I don't live in a house with a manicured garden; there are barns and wild areas, a long drive and gravel. I think she's eaten something poisonous. To feed or not? If she were older, I'd starve her for twenty -four hours but she's tiny. I make her chicken and rice. She wolfs it down.

She tries to get on the sofa in the kitchen. I am not allowing her on the furniture. I go and get the big dog bed that my last dog had distained in order to sleep on the half landing on the stairs! Nell collapses gratefully onto it and sleeps.

Visitors are coming to stay tomorrow!

Nell: More of that delicious food and I feel better. I like the big bed. She even put it in my room for bedtime. She likes me really!

Tonight, two people arrive. They also like me and I'm on my best behaviour. They give me a squeaky apple to play with. It is fun! I pounce on it and chase it and every time I touch it, it squeaks. All the people are laughing.

I am allowed in the big room with the carpet on the floor. My bed is put in there for me. She keeps taking me outside in case I want to pee. I try my best each time because then she gives me praise and, more importantly, a bit of biscuit!

Me: Hurrah! The p.p. (projectile pooing) has stopped and, although tired, Nell is looking better.

All this is just as well for family are coming to stay for five days. I am a little anxious about how Nell will behave. I've been trying to stop her from jumping up at people as it is something I hate. She can't seem to stop herself as she gets so excited. We are all practising either – lift a knee when she jumps or, turn as she's jumping, all the time saying 'No'. My brother is less stern than my sister-in-law or me and Nell has sussed him out as a pushover!

Nell: They left me all alone during the day! Why can't I go wherever they're going? She left me a treat – a chewy thing with cold stuff in the creases. It didn't last long!

Why couldn't I go with them?

Me: We went out for lunch as it was my birthday.

I left something for Nell to eat/play with.

It was a lovely day altogether and Nell was really pleased to see us when we got home.

Nell: They went out again! Without me!

Me: Nell has to get used to being left when I go out. She is very 'attached' and follows me everywhere, leaving toys, other people etc. to follow me if I move away or go into a different room. I need to be careful as she seems to have little spatial awareness and gets under my feet!

Nell: I went in that carrier again and into the car. I was good; I hardly made a sound. When we got there, she took me out and put my lead on and carried me into the vet place again.

I like the vet place. We had to wait and a lady came from behind a desk and made a big fuss of me. She said I would 'grow into' my ears! What was she trying to say? There was a strange sound from a cage thing. It wasn't a dog sound.

Later, when the nice vet lady (I really like her) had given me that tasty paste stuff, I was outside the room when I met two of my sisters! We licked each other and wagged our tails. I'd like to have spent more time catching up, comparing notes, but they hadn't been in for the tasty paste yet so we had to leave and my lead was getting caught up in legs and other leads!

Me: Last vet visit (I hope) until next year. Nell was good in the car. I carried her into the waiting room as she's gained weight and is too heavy in the carrier.

She gets made such a fuss of. The vet said if I got fed up with Nell she'd take her off my hands! The vet made me laugh – she told Nell that now she 'knew the drill' we'd not be long. The 'drill' is that I hold Nell's collar while the paste is spread and the syringe prepared. Then on the command 'go', she's allowed to clean up the paste while the vaccine is given. She didn't react to the injection at all! In the waiting room, a surprise! Her sisters! One owned by another vet and one kept by the breeder – plus, their people. Very happy pups reunited and excited getting tangled in leads and legs!

July 2022

Nell: More visitors! I love all this attention! I think these two are her friends. They all sat outside and there was lots of talking and clinking sounds. What are these noises? And – you'll think I'm so naïve about this – she never has a bowl on the floor! Nor do any of the other people visiting the house. They sit at the table after I've smelled some lovely foody smells but they don't have food in bowls on the floor. Do they never have to eat? Perhaps they're not living! Perhaps they're robots! Imagine never knowing the delights of cat poo or manure!

Me: Nell was so well behaved when my friends came to dinner. It was dinner although I didn't have to cook it. They brought it with them! Nell doesn't seem to know that we eat. I have never fed her from the table and so she doesn't sit and beg. Good!

My friends said that Nell should have been called Shadow as she follows me everywhere. I hope this shows loyalty as well as the food attachment thing!

We are all quite fascinated by Nell's wiggle; her rib cage goes one way and the back end goes the other – quite a sashay!

Nell: It was so light outside and I'd been awake for ages. I'd played with my toys, been in and out of the dog flap and was **sooo** bored.

I thought to myself 'I know I'll surprise her and decorate my room. Make it more . . .me.' So, I set to work. I know she doesn't like me chewing the edges of the carpet (which I have done and very nice it looks, too) so I looked around and then I found that I could undo the metal bit at the side of my bed. Underneath, once I'd chewed a hole in the thin layer there, I found it was filled with all this squishy stuff I could pull out. So, I did! It looked lovely, though I say so myself, spread all around my room in little puffs.

She seemed not to like it but, perhaps, she has no artistic appreciation!

Me: What a mess! I couldn't see the carpet at all!

I found myself shouting "What have you done now? Naughty!" Nell was wagging her tail. She was really pleased with herself. She had undone the zip on the cover of her bed. How? I admire the deftness. She'd chewed through the inner cover and extracted the filling in puffs to cover the floor!

Now I've to sew up both the inner cover and the zip ending so that it can't be undone, as well as clearing up the filling. Whisper this, I later laughed with a friend over this!

Nell resting on Sophie and looking at Evie

August 2022

Nell: I'm trying to be good after all I'm nearly sixteen weeks old! I want others to be proud of me like they are about those Lionesses! And, of course, 'she who must be obeyed', I want her to be proud of me especially as she feeds me. She told me today that I was a 'good dog'. I don't believe she meant it but I'm not proud and will take any praise! I had a little takeaway in the field and took it to show her. She didn't seem proud of me then!

Me: Why can't Nell stop picking up the manure from the muck spreader? I always say 'No' but she seems to think it's clever.

I'm worried that she's not clever; she doesn't appear to understand 'sit' for longer than one second. I have tried explaining to Nell that there's a difference in being adventurous – that's to be admired, - and being obedient - also to be admired. This was because she took herself off and did not appear when I called her. I found myself (I'm so ashamed of this) telling her that she's not a patch on a collie. I hope she doesn't understand because she is easier to love (and loves in return) than my 'alpha female'* collie as a pup.

*This is a quote from the agility teacher, who liked neither of us!

Nell: I'm not sure what to call her. She's not my mum. Does she speak my language? Perhaps I can just call her 'her' or 'she'. Maybe, SWMBO (she who must be obeyed).

Me: I don't really want people calling me Nell's mum. Neither am I her 'person' or her 'owner' – all right, technically I am her owner but it sounds too harsh for a sentient being like a puppy.

I'll just be me and go along with whatever anyone else calls me because, in the grand scheme, what does it matter?

Nell: I thought I'd try to play the game today. Well, I think it's quite good to show that I'm worth loving – and feeding!

I fetched the ball quite enthusiastically three or four times and then, then! she was trying to get me to 'sit' and 'stay'. I didn't want to - particularly as this time she had no treats.

I did the 'sit' thing because then she gives me a stroke and says 'Good girl'. I quite like that!

I didn't want to 'stay'. I let her step backwards two steps and then got up.

She gave me a little bit of biscuit when we went inside.

Me: What a good day for Nell. She performed both toilet actions in the field in the morning and the evening!

I decided to try to train her to sit and stay but first threw the ball a few times. She brought it back! I stopped while we were still on a roll after four retrieves.

Then I tried the sit and stay. 'Sit' was fine and I praised her but when I tried to keep her sitting while I moved back (keeping eye contact) a step or two she just got up and came to me.

I feel as though I'm not on top of this!

Last night she played by herself in the hall. After I'd put her to bed, I found she'd peed in the hall. I'm teeth gnashing!

Nell: I usually walk in the field with my friends, Benson, and Sandra. They (the humans) nagged me the whole time this evening! Why? Benson was chasing a ball and I chased him but got side-tracked by some really interesting odours. When I pick up something interesting, I'm told to sit and 'leave it'. They open my mouth and take out my delicacies. Spoil sports!

Me: Tonight, Nell excelled herself in picking up the most revolting items – with, of course, the view to eating. The first was cat poo. I felt sick making her open her mouth to drop it. The other was a very dead and very odious small vole. She was loath to give this up and I had to retrieve it from her mouth with my hand. The smell stayed on my hand despite copious washes! I thought the desiccated frog (from the stream) with the punctured belly was bad but the vole was eye-wateringly much, much worse! Will this go on forever?

Nell: What began as a heavenly day became awful. They put me behind the fence! They told me off! And not once but many, many times. Actually, behind the fence was only once but that was because I wasn't let out again until they'd finished whatever they were doing.

Whatever it was, I was only trying to help. They pulled up bits of greenery – and so did I. I even tried to eat some so that they didn't have to put it in with the other compost stuff. I found stones to move for them, putting them out of the way. I cleared up the cat poo (delicious and irresistible by the way, should you want to try it) which I know they all hate. I know this because they say 'Yuck! Yuck!'. I did some digging to help move some soil. What thanks did I get? None! Scolded and scolded and then put behind the fence. I am sulking – that'll teach 'em!

Me: This Labrador thing about eating anything, especially if it is particularly revolting, is beginning to wear me down: Today, there were four adults and a child doing some gardening – to tidy up a bit before my visitors tomorrow. I cannot tell you how many times Nell was reprimanded for finding and eating cat poo. It was making everyone feel rather queasy. I'd wanted Nell to be outside with us so that she was not excluded but this proved impossible. Later, we thought of ways to deter or punish which might change these actions of hers. We considered trying to put something in her mouth immediately after eating poo – something horrid but harmless, so that she would associate the two – and desist! Cloves of garlic were considered, lemon juice squirted into her mouth and mustard among others. Then we thought that we ought to check up to see if any were harmful to dogs. Apparently, garlic is! Who knew? My previous dog loved garlic bread when she was lucky enough to get a leftover piece. She also ate scraps from any ragu or casserole with garlic in. So, garlic is out. Mustard seems a choice but how to administer? Who would have it on them ready (this would have to be me) after an unexpected snack? Impossible. Easier to squirt lemon juice into a mouth, I think. I must research more! Nell is sulking!

Nell: I was on my best behaviour. I made myself as charming as possible just to show that I can and, let me be honest, to show her that I am lovable and a 'good dog'. I thought I'd better, after yesterday, even though I don't know what I did wrong.

She thinks I don't know about 'people food'. I do now but I choose not to show that I know because I worry that she might not feed me if I take something not put down for me. When I find crumbs on the floor, I clear them up since that is helpful. If it's one of my jobs, I'm happy to oblige.

I like being made a fuss of and today there was a surfeit of strokes and cuddles and pats. Hurrah! Some of those signs of affection even came from her. Hurrah again!

Me: Today, I appear to have a wonderfully behaved dog! What happened?

There were fourteen of us; eleven adults and three children — all relatives and some from the other side of the world – for lunch. They arrived earlier than expected but we were ready!

Nell was a paragon of virtue; she did not jump up but sat to be stroked. She did not get under anyone's feet but was friendly to all. Thankfully, the weather was kind and we ate outside. I am glad that I've told people not to feed Nell – the food was out on the table in the kitchen and people carried outside whatever they'd chosen. Nell made no attempt to sniff the table in the kitchen nor to watch as people were eating. Some, I know, would have given her titbits but, thankfully, they also obeyed the house rules! I got the impression that some think I'm very mean about these treats. I don't care! Nobody likes a dog begging when they're eating and Nell doesn't do this. I still wonder if she knows that we eat at all. She was praised profusely by me when they'd left.

Nell: I've tried bird poo. It's not so good. They leave droppings outside the back door. Now the young have gone there's not so much poo. She clears it up and wears a mask muttering something about bird flu.

Well, this evening, I saw the birds in the field when I was chasing Benson. I'm much better at running than I was so I thought I'd chase them to see who could get back to the house the fastest. I wasn't too demoralised that they got there before me. The gate was shut but I knew that they were 'in'. They were definitely our swallows. I ran back when I was called. **I love running.**

Me: Benson is so good with Nell. If she overstepped the mark, I think he'd tell Nell off but he quite good-naturedly bears her biting his ears, back legs and tail.

When we're walking in the fields, Benson chases after his ball and Nell chases after him! She rarely gets the ball but, if she does, he removes it from her mouth! Sandra bought her a soft, squeaky ball of her own so that she'd carry it – and, maybe, not pick up the muck. Benson seemed to prefer Nell's ball to his own but then she happily carried his, which is broken. She could get her mouth inside and wore it like a clown's nose! She is really not interested in retrieving a ball – maybe she just wants to make Sandra and me laugh.

Nell has a spikey ball like Benson's blue one. When Benson picked this ball up, Sandra told him off because it was – wait for it – purple and girly! We both laughed at the ridiculousness of this!

When they have no balls with them, Benson and Nell are quite happy chasing each other or exploring on their own. Well, it's Nell who explores, jumping with all four paws off the ground after moths and birds. Birds! She seemed to recognise the swallows swooping over the long grass as those who have a nest above the back door. She chased them as they flew over two fields! When she came back she looked pleased with herself – as if she'd seen them safely home - or warned them off!

Millie, Emily and Evie with Nell

September 2022

Nell: I walked outside, on the lane, with Benson. Benson ran on and I tried to catch him but I had this 'thing' strapped on. My front legs went in it and it did up on my back and that's where the lead was attached.

There were new and interesting smells on the lane; some black berries and other little black balls that were tasty.

One quad passed us and Benson sat down by Sandra. SWMBO made me sit, too. We stayed still after the quad had passed and I didn't know why until a dog ran after it. This dog didn't look at Benson or me. Rude!

She and I walked down the hill this morning. I was on the lead with the 'thing' on me. So many cars today! I sat down as I'd seen Benson do. She told me I was a 'good dog'! Then, and I was so pleased for a while, I found some old cat poo at the side of the road that needed removing – into me! Then, I was told off! Perhaps she'll make us stick to the field for our walks but she was saying something like the road wears down my sharp claws.

Me: Yesterday, I took Nell (Benson and Sandra came too) along the road to walk. I say road but it's a country lane with verges (overgrown) and banked hedges. Sandra has lent me a dog harness, for Nell, and I thought I'd try it again to see if it fits now; the few times I've tried it before, Nell could have walked out of it – and that's on the smallest setting! It fits! And it's snug. I've not noticed how much she's grown. I put the harness on half an hour before we were due to meet up and then added the lead and walked her around for a few minutes. She's not too keen but I think it's better than an ordinary collar and lead at this time – I'm sure she'll pull when Benson rushes on and I don't want her strangled!

It takes roughly an hour to walk this particular route and Nell was really quite good. She did pull a bit but also stopped to sniff and, of course, eat things on the road. Benson walks (and runs) off the lead. He's very good at coming back to sit when a car, or any other vehicle, is coming. Nell was exhausted when we got home.

Today, Nell and I went for a short road walk in the opposite direction to yesterday. Four cars passed us and, wait for this, Nell sat each time as I tucked her into the jungle of the verge. Something learned from Benson? I hope so. Maybe, just maybe, she'll also be able to walk off the lead one day.

Nell: I've discovered something I'm allowed to take and eat and not be told off! These tasty fruits are growing all along the fences in the fields. Blackberries!

I had a wonderful time with the tall man and the three girls. They picked blackberries and so did I. The girls were a bit moany about the stinging nettles but I'm not bothered by them. The man told the girls to make their hands and arms into slinky snakes to avoid the nettles. I just went straight in but I could also eat any that the girls dropped. Win, win!

I was very tired after this.

Me: My son took the girls blackberrying in the fields and Nell went too. They picked so many! They are taking them home and are intent on making blackberry crumble. Nell, apparently, has found a taste for them. I discovered this to be the truth when we walked in the field later – she sniffed where the girls had stood and then began eating the berries she could reach. She looks for them every day now! A 'take away' I don't mind her having!

Nell: I love those wellies that are outside. She lets me play with them but she doesn't seem too happy when I, very cleverly, get them through the dog flap. Why? If I can play with them outside, why can't I play inside with them? The little wellies have been thrown away. I'm not surprised since I had chewed great holes in them. They were prettier than the big ones. They had some sort of animal on. Not dogs, though.

Me: I think I have, unwittingly, made Nell have a rubber fetish! I allowed her to play with the old wellies that have not yet been thrown away. (Why have I got all this 'stuff' hanging around?) When she was tiny the small wellies my granddaughters wore were ideal for her to toss and throw around outside. Then she turned her attention to the adult ones and that was still fine. For some inexplicable reason she has never touched mine which are housed just outside the back door, under roof cover. Good. Then, she began to bring these 'toys' inside through the dog flap! Each time she does this, I throw them back outside. Well, the little wellies have been chewed; she's managed to make great holes in the leg parts. At least, fortunately, she doesn't eat the pieces. However, she has begun to chew the edges off the utilitarian carpet which covers most of the floor in the boot room. She doesn't eat these pieces either but, in order to get to a fresh area, she is strong enough to fold back whole bits of carpet to see if she can chew the backing! Often this involves moving her bed out of the way. I call it 'doing a Pickfords' which just shows how old I am! And, when I was carrying the umbrella on one very wet walk, she was trying to eat the handle – made of rubber, of course!

Nell: Through soaking wet grass is fine, I can do that, but the rain was absolutely stinging me! I sat down, refusing to carry on. She had an umbrella thing and is dry on her head but I notice that her legs are getting soaked above her wellies.

When we got in, she has fun with me by rubbing me with a towel. She is contradictory telling me to 'sit' and then 'up'. I wish she'd make up her mind, so I roll over onto my back!

Me: We've been so lucky with the weather until now. I know that the ground needs this rain but now I have the problem of 'wet dog'. I have a lot of old towels - a consequence of not throwing away old things! I can use them to dry Nell although getting her to stay still proves difficult. I'd like her to stand so that I can dry down each leg and underneath her as well as her head, ears and back. Nell, of course, rolls over and thinks the towel is a toy.

Nell: **I thought she'd left me!** She went out and left me a chew. This is nothing unusual as she goes shopping and to other places but this was different. Lunch time came – no food. I was worried. Was she okay? Is she ever coming back? What would I do if she never came back? Who would feed me? Is she fed up with me?

Some paint had flaked off a tiny bit of wall in my room. I licked where it came from and it was quite nice so I chewed a bit of it to keep body and soul together. It was only a very small bit. When I heard the car, I was so relieved and excited. We had a big cuddle and she fed me.

Things are quieter with just the two of us. I try to keep her entertained in the evenings with my toys because she doesn't seem to have any of her own.

She gives me the best strokes – she loves those ears that I'm growing into! – and cuddles.

Aah!

Me: Now that my grandchildren are back at school and summer visitors have gone, Nell and I are on our own a great deal more of the time. We are settling into a routine which usually involves walking the fields each evening with Sandra and Benson. I have also been taking Nell for a short field walk in the morning and a short road walk at lunch time as we need the 'on the lead' practise. On her own, Nell is walking better on the lead and (I'll write this tentatively) not picking up anything like so many bits of acorn or squashed manure.

I went clothes shopping one day and was much later back than I'd expected. Nell had obviously been quite anxious at the length of time I'd been away. It was only later that I found the small 'hole' in the plastered wall in the boot room. I felt so guilty about being out for so long but I was also cross. She's not touched it since.

In the evenings, Nell has a habit of bringing more toys into the sitting room to play. Is she trying to detract my attention from the television or just entertain? This is also a time when she rests her head on the edge of the sofa, inviting a cuddle.

Aah!

October 2022

Nell: I was afraid of the huge, noisy machines that went in and out of our fields. I ran back through the dog flap. I don't think I'm a wuss – just being sensible. When they left, we walked in the fields and I could see for miles! I don't need to jump up and leap over the very long grass anymore.

I used to flush out and chase the crane flies from the long grass but now that it's shorter I have a new occupation. I have found some really interesting animals to take and show her how clever I am. They are not alive – that might have made it more fun. I think the machines killed them and now I know I was sensible to go inside! These little creatures don't seem to please her. She makes me sit and opens my mouth to take them out. I had thought that maybe she wanted them for herself – to eat – but I found out by her response of 'ugh!' that that wasn't the case. She is practising her throwing skills by tossing them into the hedge. No thanks for me, no praise about how clever I am. Is she never satisfied?

Me: The fields have been scalped for the second silage cut. It makes it so much easier for dog walking; no high knee lifting over long lush grass and Nell doesn't come back quite so soaking wet in the mornings. I'd thought that she might now bring back the ball on the rope toy as she can race across the short grass and see where it lands. No. She gets excited and races to it and stands over it with that look– 'if you want it, come and get it yourself!'

I met someone I know in the supermarket (as you do) and we began a conversation about puppies – of which she seems to be quite an expert. She recommends a collar with the lead, rather than the harness, as Labradors have their strength in their shoulders and need to be taught not to pull by having pressure on their throats/necks. She also suggested hiding tiny pieces of meat outside for Nell to 'find' to improve her scenting skills. I shall not be doing this since it is unnecessary; this week alone she has scented and carried in her mouth to me, from the fields, five voles, four tiny shrews and a frog. These were all dead stock rather than livestock and some of them were very dead indeed! I know that she has something by her very pleased manner and the tell-tale tiny tails hanging from her mouth. She doesn't drop these offerings but seems quite content for me to remove them and throw them into the hedge. I have started using a tissue for this operation and can confirm that five thorough hand washes do not remove the disgusting smell from the very dead!

Nell: I think there are rabbits in the bank by the fence in the big field. Such an intoxicating scent! I was tracking it when she stopped still. She was looking down the field and was quite mesmerised by what I caught sight of out of the corner of my eye – a pretty huge animal – not a dog! If it had been a dog, I'd have run up and made friends. She was whispering to me about staying still when another big animal joined the first. I carried on with my rabbit scenting. She mystifies me. Did she want me to chase those animals away? Or retrieve them for her? I know my limitations!

Me: This morning, as we were right up by the fence in the top field, a deer came out of the gateway from the little field. It stood still and so did I. I looked at Nell who was sniffing the grass along by the fence. She was oblivious to all else. I whispered to her to stay still – to no avail. Then, quite magically, a second deer joined the first. They both stood for a few seconds. I know that they'd seen and scented me but they were unconcerned. The first turned and retraced her steps but the second calmly trotted down the field following the fence line.

Having no one else to talk to, I said to Nell "Did you see, or even notice? Can you scent their trails?" She did not respond. She continued sniffing the grass and even when we were along the same line as the second deer, by the fence, she showed no interest, no reaction!

Nell: I pushed on the entertainment button on Friday when some people came over. They had dinner (it smelled delicious) and then went into the sitting room. I'm allowed in there all the time now. I sat by the visitors and put my head on their knees – not both at the same time! - and they cuddled and stroked me. Well, I have to take every opportunity for affection. I'm not too proud to squirm and simper. In fact, I'm not proud at all!

Those little girls came over and brought Sophie with them. I was so excited. We went into the field to play and Benson came to join us! We chased the ball on the rope and played tug-of-war with it! My mouth hurts. I think it's bleeding but I'm still playing! I walked Benson to his gate as he was alone.

Those big machines are in again but this time they smell really lovely . . .

She put the lead on me and took me to Benson's. I haven't been before and on the way round the house I was a bit afraid. She pulled me along! But then, there was Benson and I was free and we ran around. We went into a field which had interesting smells. I was told off (yet again!) by two people because I was eating the tasty things on the ground. It didn't stop me! I was taking my chances when I could! Then, then, we went down a little steep bit and Benson went splash! Splash! Through some water and into another field. I followed! I jumped into the water and out again. I've never been in water before. I was praised and encouraged to go in again. Benson chased sticks in the deeper bit of water. I was cautious of the deep part. On the way back, I saw some white animals in the distance but they didn't run over so I just carried on with Benson. I had a great time!

Me: Some friends of mine came to dinner on Friday evening. Nell seems to know how to be on her best behaviour (and cutest) when I have guests. We went into the sitting room. Nell put her head on each person's knee in turn, inviting a stroke or a cuddle. She licked their fingers. It wasn't until after eleven p.m. that she crashed out for a sleep!

On Sunday, more visitors! My daughter, her partner, my granddaughters and their dog, Sophie, came over. As soon as Nell realised the car was stopping and the doors were opening, she was quivering with excitement. She raced over, jumping up (and, of course, making the youngest cry) and then racing with Sophie into the field. In fact, we all went into the field and let the dogs race around and we threw the ball on a rope for them. This was not very successful until we were suddenly joined by Benson(!) who loves chasing the ball. Nell chased him and even chased the ball – and brought it back – herself! Result! I took Benson home as he had taken it upon himself to visit. Nell has blood in her mouth and we think she's lost a puppy tooth! We all wonder if there is a dog tooth fairy and what the fairy would leave!

Oh! I knew it would happen. After silaging, there is always the fields being covered in farmyard 'muck'. It is smelly and lands in large clumps from the muck spreader. It will be like a magnet for Nell. I ring Sandra and we agree to walk in her fields – another new experience for Nell – as there's sheep! Nell was dubious about going round the side of Sandra's house but as soon as she saw Benson she was off and running with him. They charged across the lawn but then into the fields. The sheep were out of the way but their droppings were an absolute draw for Nell who left chasing Benson to devour them. Both Sandra and I said 'No' but she took no notice. You'd think that, by now, she'd know what 'no' means and that she is out of favour!

At the bottom of the fields is the river. It's the same river that runs along the bottom of my fields but my land is all fenced from it. Benson loves the water and crossed it to get to another field. Nell jumped right into it and across. Benson chased sticks into the water and Nell did the same but was hesitant about the deeper areas. What a busy day for Nell!

(The aftermath was, of course, a lot of dog poo to clear up the next morning – the result of sheep poo eating!)

Nell: I was having a little chew of teddy. My teeth are irritating me and the softness of teddy is, somehow, comforting. Imagine my surprise when one of teddy's eyes came away in my mouth! I took it to show her. (I thought, at first, that it was a worrying tooth that had come out.)

"Oh!" she said. "It's teddy's eye. Now, she'll only have one, as though she's winking. Don't free the other or else she'll be blind." Did she think I'd done it on purpose? I hadn't but imagine my horror when she put the eye in the bin! I'd thought she might sew it back on. Poor teddy, suturing required.

Me: Nell came to me with that 'look'. The 'look' says 'I have something in my mouth.' We were in the house. Nell never drops things from her mouth; her game to me is for her to sit and let me open her mouth and then to take, or shake out, the object. It was a brown plastic eye. In her puppy 'goody bag' from the breeder Nell had a lovely blanket and a teddy, both pink and both have survived much washing. Now teddy has only one eye! In her 'loving' of the teddy, Nell had managed to remove one eye without mammoth surgery – somehow, there is no hole, no innards hanging out!

Nell: <u>She was choking me</u>! I hated it! And – I could not catch up with Benson or go any faster. What has she put on me?

When a great big monster vehicle passed, I was really scared. I wanted to run away and tried backing away but she made me stay still and sit by her while the vehicle made a rushing sound, passing us.

I found I could still stop and sniff the verges and she waited for me. If I go slower, it is much better and she and Sandra say 'Good dog'. I was even praised for going to the loo!

On the way back, I think I was getting the hang of it. I sat when a car went by us and was praised. I saw big animals in a field and there was a gate to stop them from coming out. Good, because they were walking towards me!

We seemed to be out for a long time and I was really tired when we got home – and thirsty. She said it was called 'a walk'.

Me: I put the half-choke collar on Nell to walk along the lane with Sandra and Benson. Benson ran on ahead and, of course, Nell pulled to try and catch up. She is much easier to control than when she has a harness on and she stays on my side rather than walking in front of me. She's picked up a few acorns but dropped them again and has had her first up close view of cattle.

She got better at walking more slowly as the evening wore on. She saw how Benson came back to sit by the side of Sandra (and the road) whenever there was a car or tractor and began to sit herself without prompting. We'll need to do more of this as the fields can't be walked for a while.

Nell: What is she doing to me now? She's forcing my face into some mesh thing that covers my eyes. She is trying to sound sweet. I put up my paw to push it off. It goes nowhere. She takes it off, laughing. Laughing! Then she puts it on again but this time I can see. She smiles and says "let's go in the field!" I'm ready for that but this thing is irritating. I try to get it off by rubbing my face against the grass, first one side, then the other. It doesn't move. I try this over and over, all the time we're walking round the field, rubbing one whole side of my body, too, to get this thing off. It stays on. When we get back she puts the hose on me because there's some of the muck from the field on me.

She hates me!!

Me: I have succumbed! Worn out with the constant 'No, Nell' as yet another disgusting object disappears, at speed, into Nell's mouth and by my having to remove said object (yuck!), I have bought a muzzle. My thinking is that for a few weeks/months of wearing it she might grow out of this scavenging habit.

The buying of the muzzle was strange, a bit surreal! I found myself asking the assistant in the pet shop, sotto voce, - almost a whisper as if it was a sex shop (I don't think I've ever been in a sex shop but I imagine there's some furtiveness to it!)- "Do you sell muzzles?" Equally complicit in the whisper she replied. "Yes. I'll get you a selection to choose from." To add to the analogy, the muzzles were towards the back of the shop – not on the public display shelves!

The assistant then asked what it was for! Duh – a dog! Why? She wanted to know. When I said that Nell was a Labrador she smiled and when I said she'd been trying to eat acorns she immediately responded with "But they're poisonous!" Much as I find it annoying that Nell tries to eat acorns, I found myself being protective towards her – after all, she doesn't know they're poisonous.

A size three was purchased from those shown to me. One, rejected immediately by me, was like a vast, strapped box shape. Nell is definitely not vicious. This muzzle looked like it belonged on a huge Rottweiler. Sorry, Rottweilers. The helpful assistant suggested that maybe I should be training Nell not to pick up 'delicacies' by – wait for it – turning her round and retracing our steps when Nell stops to examine the titbits on offer and rewarding with treats. I shall do neither. Doesn't the assistant realise just how quickly Nell hoovers up? There'd be no time! And, we'd be constantly turning round and going in the opposite direction! I don't really agree with rewarding with food treats too often but I may have to reconsider this ideal of mine!

To continue the 'suggestive' analogy from before, I told Nell that I'd bought her the fishnet rather than the lisle version as I fastened it on her (upside down at first so that she couldn't see!) which made me laugh, if not her. She gave me a look.

She hates me!!

Nell: The muzzle! I cannot get it off! I spend my whole time in the field trying to get it off. It doesn't matter that she tells me that it is camouflaged against my face, that I am interestingly veiled. Such soft soaping! It is horrible and I hate it! <u>I shall not give in</u>!

Me: The muzzle has not proved particularly successful; Nell can just about pick up an acorn (but not chew it) but, much worse, she constantly rubs her face against any surface in order to try and dislodge it. She has rubbed skin from her nose and mouth. It seemed such a good solution but now I doubt the result is worth the anguish (mine!).

Nell: Freedom! But not total freedom – there's always a proviso and it is that the muzzle – I'm going to use that ugly word, not 'mask' – is a threat to me to behave! Don't tell her but as punishment goes it isn't too bad as she takes it off after a while and I can go back to doing what I do well – sniff and explore with my nose and mouth! This is what my senses are for!

Me: I've thought a lot about 'the muzzle problem'. I've decided that I have to compromise! I am going to carry the 'mask'- as I now call it - showing it to Nell at the beginning of a walk and, if she picks up anything, I will put it on her! I will keep it on for a few minutes, then remove it to see if a lesson has been learned . . .

Nell: I was off the lead! I followed Benson, sniffing and running off ahead. Such fun! I covered a lot of ground. Then, Benson picked up a long stick and teased me with it when I tried to get it or help carry it. He did let me help him after a time and we both carried it along the lane. For some reason Sandra and 'she who must be obeyed' were laughing all the time.

Me: Another first for Nell! Today, a Sunday, I very bravely (for me) let Nell off the lead with Benson along the lane when we went for a walk. I knew that she would follow Benson and she is very, very good at coming back when called. Off they set; he leading, she following, ready to play. It was quiet along the lane with no traffic at all – thank goodness!

Benson decided to show Nell the stick carrying game. The longer the stick the better. Mind your legs, you humans! Nell threw herself into this game with vigour, trying to get some purchase on the stick too. Benson did the turning trick just as she was about to get hold but she didn't give up and, eventually, they ended up both holding it in their mouths, prancing along like an ill-matched pair of ponies. I cannot explain how much laughter it caused Sandra and myself. What a tonic!

Nell: Another person has arrived and she has bags so I think she is staying. She makes a big fuss of me and I make a big fuss of her. She gives me a new chewy toy and both humans have fun putting food into it for me to find and eat. This is my kind of play!

I am given a new food bowl. At first, I am rather dubious about it – I know that I can eat the food inside but I can't just plough in as I usually do. I have to chase the food around, some of it flicks out onto the carpet and I hurriedly clear it up. I don't want them to eat it! I am excited about the whole thing and feel as though I've had a workout! (I've heard her say this when she's done her exercises.)

Then, they play in/out with me through yet another dog flap. They give me a tiny treat each time I arrive on one side or the other. Then they close the door and leave me to it. I go in and out, in and out, but they are not there with any more treats! What happened? I did as they wanted and then they ignored me! However, it is fun and I now have two doorways which are just for me since they don't use them! At night they lock this second dog flap so that I stay in my room. I know because I tried it and it wouldn't budge!

Me: I am going to London for a few days

 A friend of mine from 'up country' – as they say in Devon - Hampshire, in fact, is coming to stay to house and, mainly, dog sit. Fortunately, she likes dogs!

Nell is thrilled to have someone else to entertain. She is given a new toy to be filled with treats for chewing and licking. We try it out and Nell enjoys finding the bits of kibble stuck into cheese paste. When my friend and I go out, she buys Nell a new food bowl – one divided into circular sections which is designed to slow down her extra fast devouring of food! And so, Nell learns two new things. The first is how to use the new bowl. Amazingly, the food takes at least three or four minutes to eat rather than the usual thirty seconds I am used to. If any pieces fall out onto the carpet, she hurriedly tidies them up, her tail – well, actually, her whole body, wagging, moving with excitement all the while! We are enthralled watching her and I am relieved that, at last, she'll get to digest her food properly.

The second thing we teach her is to use the second dog flap which leads from the boot room into the main house. I had kept this flap locked before now and the whole door closed at night. Now that autumn is upon us the door needs to be closed during the day too and so Nell had to learn how to get in and out. I'd tried to encourage her on my own but she was scared. My friend and I resurrected the same trick used by my granddaughters, with one each side of the flap calling to her. We rewarded her with tiny treats. She soon got the hang of it! She spent ages going in and out on her own, showing off her new trick!

Nell: <u>She's left me again</u>! I sensed something was up when she was putting things into bags.   Someone came to collect her one morning and she was gone! Her friend is still here. She walks me, feeds me – all as usual – and makes a fuss of me. She walks me in the fields and dries me with a towel just like SWMBO (she who must be obeyed). In the evening, we both snuggle in the sitting room and during the day she does things with big needles and small needles! I think it's 'sewing'.

I had such a shock one day. Her voice (SWMBO) was in the hall but she wasn't there! I looked for her and began to get anxious. Her friend did something that made the voice sound again. I didn't like it.

There are big scary things in the new, little field. They are huge and black, dotted about on the grass. I was told that they were okay, not to be frightened, but I didn't want to get too close. I was encouraged to approach them and they didn't bite or run away – they just stayed still. Maybe they're okay but there's no need to chance it unless I have to.

Me: While I was away, the new little field was cut, turned, baled and wrapped as haylage. My friend told me that Nell was fearful of the black, wrapped 'monsters' or 'animals' in the field and that she'd gone up patting them to show Nell that they didn't attack or bite!

Nell: She's back! She's really pleased to see me and her friend but I can tell that there's something wrong. She's shivery and tired. I'd best behave.

She gets up as usual and takes me out in the field but she's not the same. What is wrong? I can't do anything but I am quiet with my best behaviour. I don't want her to go away again!

The friend stays for another day and then leaves. I'll have to look after SWMBO, but how can I? I'm only a six-month-old puppy!

Sandra and Benson appear each evening and take me in the field but SWMBO takes me each morning.

Me: I began to feel 'not quite right' on the journey back from London. I hadn't realised quite how much I missed certain things in London – some of them small -the fantastic Turkish supermarket near our hotel and some bigger - the Cezanne exhibition at the Tate Modern, James Taylor at the Apollo, both wonderful – my kind of culture fix! I had missed Nell though and the wide open spaces of my part of Devon.

I was aching and had a temperature. I thought I was just tired after all the walking and walking, including the stairs in the hotel! I did a test. Covid! The timing was wrong for me to have picked it up in London - I'd taken it with me and brought it back as it began to develop. My travelling friend didn't get it but Val, my house/dog sitter friend took it back to Hampshire. It was no worse than the 'flu but causing 'brain fog'. I managed to take Nell out each morning and my wonderful neighbour, Sandra, walked Nell and Benson in the early evenings. Nell was good company as I swallowed paracetamol and lay reading on the sofa. A friend had said, when I'd announced that I was getting a dog, 'it's another heartbeat in the house'. When not feeling well, there's nothing quite like that not being alone feeling. Hurrah for that other heartbeat!

Nell: Sandra has told me off so much this evening. Why? She has been taking me into her fields and I run and chase with Benson. This evening, I knew where to go and raced round ahead of Sandra. There was a bird to chase and I nearly caught it! I got a few feathers and that's when Sandra told me off! Then I was told off for racing around – or so it seemed! I don't seem to be able to do anything right!

Me: I'm ashamed of Nell. She went racing round Sandra's house and found Sandra's last remaining hen in the open run. She went in, coming out with a mouthful of feathers! Chastised, she then became a 'devil dog' (Sandra's words) for the rest of the walk. Sandra was still cross with Nell when they returned. I know that Nell will no longer realise what Sandra's anger is about. This is always a dilemma – how long can 'punishment' go on for?

Nell: Each evening, now that she seems better, we walk in the fields with Sandra and Benson. The grass is quite long – as though those big machines hadn't cut it at all! I encourage Benson to run with me by picking up sticks – if I can find them. Sometimes he does play and sometimes he goes off sniffing around on his own.

Me: Back to normal, whatever that is! We are walking my fields with Sandra and Benson each evening. Nell always tries to get Benson to chase her and, sometimes, he does! Nell doesn't realise that, if you do the seven dog years to one of human's, he's seventy and she's three and a half! Soon, the clocks will change and we'll only be able to walk together at weekends, when Sandra isn't working. Soon there might be sheep in the fields eating down the grass which has carried on growing this year. That will be interesting . . .

Stop press! The hen lives!

Nell and Sophie

November 2022

Nell: Those two friends came again and had dinner with SWMBO. Then we all went into the sitting room and I enjoyed being the centre of attention by making myself lovable. Then, her friend, Helen, played with squeaky monkey. I don't mind sharing my toys and, obviously, Helen has none of her own. She was doing a weird thing with monkey; sometimes it went behind her legs and sometimes it appeared at one side or the other. I watched, bemused. Is she doing this for me? If so, she could have saved her energy because I am not a baby. Humans are very odd – I don't understand them at all!

Me: My friends came to dinner and I actually cooked this time – although not, in my view, successfully. We ate it anyway!

Nell is so clever! Visitors mean 'best behaviour'. When we went into the sitting room, she did her 'go to each person and act endearingly' thing, getting cuddles and strokes from all. Helen was given, by Nell, a toy — squeaky monkey (not in pristine condition as it has been dragged inside and out, mouthed and chewed, and is not washable!). Helen decided to play with it, teasing Nell by hiding the toy behind her legs, playing 'which side will it appear on?' — and then moving it along. Nell watched, somewhat quizzically.

Nell: The tall man came with his daughter. The girl had made me a card — quite sweet really but not edible! She tried to teach me catch, with a ball. I did catch it once and was much praised. Don't they realise that if they threw food, I'd catch it every time?

We walked in the fields. I loved that; I could chase one of them, walk with one, follow one- and it had stopped raining!

Me: Two for Sunday lunch – my son and granddaughter. Nell had a big fuss made of her and was played with.

We walked in the fields before they had to go home.

Nell loves these times. I sometimes feel sad for her that she only has me for much of the time since she is so sociable. However, I'm glad for me!

Nell: She's been taking me along the lane with the lead on. And, we seem to be going out earlier and to bed later! She pulls me back on the lead and says "No!" when I am racing to follow an interesting scent. There are so many new smells along the lane. Sometimes, we meet a big collie called Ben. I don't think he likes me as he always growls and barks at me even though I am being enthusiastically friendly towards him. He's the only dog who does this to me – is it his way of saying hallo?

Me: Now it's dark early, as the clocks have changed, Nell thinks it's bedtime at seven or eight o'clock! She keeps looking at me as if to say, why are you still up?'

I've been walking her either in the field or along the lane to practise her being on the lead. She is better at not eating along the verges!

Sometimes, we meet Brian and his dog, Ben. Ben is very dubious of Nell and warns her off. Luckily, she takes the hint. Brian says that Ben isn't keen on being 'bounced' by Tiggerish Nell; he doesn't like lively puppies jumping up at him. Ben isn't an old dog.

Nell: We are not walking in the fields! We go into the paddock – fun! – and along the lane.

Yesterday, she took me to the gate into the field and I thought 'hooray, we're going in' but no! There were already some animals in there. How dare they! They must be the reason we don't go in – she's organised lodgers on my land! Huh! And – she showed them to me – rubbing my nose into the fact that they have my space!

Me: Sheep have arrived to eat down the grass that has continued growing in the fields. At the moment, the sheep are all in the bottom field and are making a good job of munching the very long grass which cannot be cut on the slope down to the river.

I am taking Nell into the very overgrown paddock – off the lead – and along the lane on the lead. She's quite funny in the paddock; she leaps over the tussocks of two-year-old grass. This area is also not smooth; there are dips and bumps making her jump quite high as she chases a ball or stick. I'm not so keen as my wellies sometimes get caught in ankle snatching coils of long grass or, worse, brambles. Still, the high knee steps must be good for my legs!

Nell: Good! More people! We all worked outside in the lovely sunny weather. I did much more than the humans I was helping. I was back and forth wearing my paws out carrying important bits of wood and greenery. Exhausting!

Of course, as all visitors do, they all went out and left me alone. But I was made a fuss of when they got back. I love having visitors; they are fun and when they leave I try to make SWMBO happy by making a fuss of her. After all, she feeds me!

The humans were so coarse one evening; someone had whiffy wind and they all looked at me as the guilty party. I gave them my most disdainful look and walked out! I didn't want to stay in the room with that odour!

One evening, she took me into the little field as those other animals had gone into the top field. It was very, very windy and raining, so we went quickly. I might like those other animals as they had left me some dainty titbits to try. She said "No" but I sneaked a few!

Me: My sister and brother-in-law have arrived for a four or five day visit. Nell is so thrilled to have more people to make a fuss of her – and they do! My brother-in-law likes to be outside and has cut back the shrubs and demolished the gooseberry bushes! My sister and I began the leaf clearing down the drive although the trees have not lost all their leaves yet. Nell was out with us and thoroughly enjoyed going backwards and forwards from drive to garden area, helping by picking up twigs and cuttings and redistributing them elsewhere! The weather was a delight, too.

Nell, occasionally, releases those 'dog smells' which, for some reason, are usually in the evening. We all remonstrated with her one evening as we were 'down wind'. The look that she gave us was so funny; it said 'don't blame me. I can smell it too and I think it was you.' Then, she got up and walked, nose in the air aristocratically and condescendingly, out. So funny!

Nell knew exactly when our visitors were leaving; she has begun to recognise cases and bags being carried in or out and associates them with arriving or leaving humans. She has been bought some chews (for teeth) and a brush for her coat. The brush is now important as she is moulting short black hair all over the floors – it seems to be the only stuff that is emptied from the vacuum cleaner!

Nell: Two days of walking with my friend, Benson, again. We walked, well, ran along the road and I was off the lead, like him. Sandra came and her sister as well as SWMBO.

Benson had a ball to carry and I tried to get it off him on the first day. When he put it down so that he could sniff in the hedgerow, I picked it up and ran off with it so that he had to chase me.

On the second day, he didn't have the ball but he picked up a long stick (from the hedges being cut) and we carried it together some of the time and he teased me with it at other times. We left it behind at some point but collected it again on the return journey for another game.

I don't feel quite myself. I want to stay close to SWMBO and cuddle. Something is happening to me. . .

Oh! I am having to clean myself and a bit of the floor. Nobody told me about this.

Me: Sandra's sister was here for the weekend and we walked with them on Saturday and with Sandra on Sunday. Benson and Nell were so pleased to see each other and played 'chase who has managed to get the ball.' Benson seems to put it down on purpose for Nell to pick up and run off with. He's so good with her.

On Sunday, no ball, so both dogs played with the long stick that Benson managed to pull out from the hedge trimming. Sandra and I were laughing at their antics. We wondered if we could use them as stick collectors – for use as kindling. 'Kindling will be delivered by dog. No distance too far, no stick too long, friendly service' was to be our advertising slogan – and all environmentally friendly. We thought better of it when the stick was abandoned!

Oh! Poor Nell! Seven months old and there, on the tiles in my kitchen, the tell-tale red spots of blood from her first season – 'in oestrus' it says on the internet. (I had to check that I hadn't inadvertently nicked myself before looking at Nell's rear end.) I hope all the local male dogs have been 'done' and I'm almost glad that it is raining – washing away her scent from our walks. She's being very affectionate – a bit 'needy' – towards me; always by my side or under the table if I sit at it. I'm giving her cuddles and comfort.

I have been taking Nell in the little paddock to stretch her legs. It is fenced and 'safe' from other dogs. Unfortunately, she'll not have her usual amount of exercise. (Only Benson has been neutered, I discover.)

Day one of running with the pack.

Nell: SWMBO and I waited at the end of our drive for Sandra and Benson. She had been telling me that we'd be going out for a walk soon as we'd only been outside for a five minute toilet break earlier in the morning. Wow! Not just

Benson but two others! We all said hallo. We were excited and running around quickly. Benson had one of his balls but he put it down by the gates and I showed how quick I could be by picking it up speedily and keeping hold of it for a long way along the lane. We were all racing – well, not the humans! – back and forth, into the ditches, along the verges. Benson seemed less interested in getting the ball from me than the other two. Did we move! I was dodging and darting, running the gamut of trying to pass the others who sort of lined up in front of me. Part way along, Archie got the ball and we all chased him! We were in and out of very deep puddles (in gateways) and muddy banks on either side of the lane.

On the return journey, Benson picked up a stick and he and I played our usual game of me trying to carry it with him but this didn't last for long. Marley got the ball and carried it most of the way back although Benson got it for a bit. That was only fair as it's his ball! Good sharing from Benson.

Me: Sandra has her son's two dogs staying for a few days. They are both male and, like Benson, have been neutered so I am letting Nell run off the lead with them so that they can protect her from any amorous dogs and so that they all get lots of exercise! They certainly got that! Off they ran, four dogs in fully excited mode, racing along our country lane. The weather has been, and still is, awful; heavy rain showers and really windy. There's mud and decomposing leaves on the verges/banks and standing water across the lane – deep in some gateways. The dogs don't care; they leap and career over and through it until they are muddy and soaked, stopping occasionally to drink from a puddle.

On the way back, there is some slight slowing down. The ball is still being sought by some and there is still play chasing going on.

My dog towels will be soaked and filthy after drying Nell but what a wonderful time for her to have had.

Sandra and I have been entertained too. There's a repeat performance tomorrow!

Day two of running with the pack.

Nell: Today I waited at the end of the drive and wondered if Benson would be alone or with the other two. I was thrilled that there were three of them again today. I got the ball! I carried it for absolutely ages and, when the others were fed up with chasing me, I teased them by flaunting the ball in their faces. I wasn't going to give it up but SWMBO said I was selfish. I still kept it!

Me: Nell knew the score today. She was straight in on the ball and excitedly carried it for almost the whole walk. She teased the others by showing the ball to them and then racing off with it or tearing around our legs. There was so much running and chasing that it was fun to watch.

Day three of running with the pack

Nell: Hurrah! All the boys were there today. Yesterday, I had to walk, really early, on the lead and then, later, in the paddock. I sulked a bit! I like to keep her on her toes! But, today, we were off! I didn't get the ball but I ran and ran. I jumped, splashed in puddles – and mud! – and tried to get the ball. When I wasn't successful, I went after one of the others to play with me. The one I chose was the same shape as me but a different colour.

When we got home, she put the hose on me! I wasn't that muddy!

Me: Yesterday, I was going to be out for most of the day so I took Nell out very early. Today, we met up again with the 'gang'. Benson is by far the oldest of the three 'boys', the other two being under three years old. There's a lot of energy which needs to be expended on racing and chasing, sniffing and jumping. One dog, Marley, was lucky enough to get the ball and kept it for the entire journey. Benson, as the 'elder statesman' of the gang, led the way and was quite diffident about the ball today – not a surprise since they'd all already been for one walk and it was still only nine thirty! What causes Sandra and I to laugh is the apparent glances that these dogs give each other from time to time – sometimes haughty, sometimes mischievous! We contemplated using them as huskies should we get snow but they are mismatched in height!

Day four of running with the pack

Nell: I was so thrilled when we stopped by our gate at the end of the drive; it meant that we were waiting for the gang. And then, there they were! All of them, not just Benson. We were off immediately, the ball being carried by Marley as we started off. We were called back when we got too far in front of the humans – they like to be able to see us, especially if the lane bends, I've noticed. Although the day before had been dry and sunny, we were soon filthy. I hope she doesn't put the hose on me again! I didn't like it – too cold! We all have turns carrying the ball and being chased for it. A great way to start the day!

In the house, she keeps looking at the floor and wiping up things. It keeps her busy!

For some reason I have to keep peeing. I drink a lot when I return from a walk but this seems constant.

Me: Sandra's son's dogs are here for the final day of their stay. We both think that Benson will be glad of the respite as this isn't the only walk of the day – they'll all be in Sandra's fields later!

Nell was quivering with excitement when she realised that we were waiting for the gang again. They all had their usual, immediate, hurried greetings and the shooting off up the hill while Sandra and I walked rather more sedately than their crazy running. We had to call them back since the lane bends and we didn't want them out of sight in case there was traffic! I sense that some readers of this will be wryly smiling and others puzzled so I'll explain that this is a single car width country lane. During the whole walk only one van passed and all the dogs came and sat on the verge, waiting for it to go by. Some drivers do not slow down so we have to be on our guard, listening for vehicles, in order to call the dogs to us.

I was going to hose Nell down when we got home but the rain started to become really heavy, so I cleaned her with all the dog towels which were then consigned to the washing machine!

Nell does not clear up after herself while her 'season' is going on – except for personal hygiene/grooming. I find I am on 'spot control' with my kitchen roll a great deal of the time as she regards me with a look that says 'what are you doing? I haven't pee'd.' Only another ten or so more days of this to go . . .

I've read that female dogs pee loads more when in season to attract males. Nell is doing this. The hussy!

Nell: We seem to be going out earlier and earlier – sometimes it is quite dark – not quite pitch black but only just light enough to see the edges of the road! I don't know what's wrong with her! And, she keeps me on the lead, quite tightly by her side. Why? I still enjoy it even though there's just the two of us. Sometimes, she stands still and looks about her. I heard this phrase 'communing with nature' -is this what she does? What does it mean? She also takes me in the paddock and treads down the long grass. She throws sticks for me and I get them to chew bits off – not to eat, that would be silly, too many splinters. She tries to get the stick but she doesn't run holding it with me like Benson.

She talks to those big white animals in our fields – and sometimes quite crossly! I look at them through the gates but she calls me back. When I look at them, they run away! Why? I'm not fierce – I'd like to play (especially chase, my speciality).

Me: On our own, I decide to go out early with Nell to avoid meeting other dogs – we should be coming up to the 'dangerous' time in Nell's season. I've told her that there will be absolutely no puppies on my watch. I believe I said "Don't even think about it". She just looks at me, not understanding, but it makes me smile. As we walk along in the almost-but-not-quite-darkness, I sing quietly to myself pop songs of old! There's no one to hear but I'm quiet all the same. The rain has stopped these last few days and I am thrilled to watch the sun rising above the outline of stark winter trees. I love the shapes that dark branches make against the sky and fields.

In the paddock I attempt to give Nell more exercise by throwing sticks, or her toys, for her to retrieve. No joy. She's now used to getting the object and running away with it for the other dogs to chase! She thinks I'll do the same!

We don't go in the fields because of the sheep. One has been on my lawn for two mornings running. How? I decide to go out and confront her, to see where she goes back in. Under the field gate is the answer! It already has a metal sheep hurdle attached beneath it but this wily ewe has found a corner where she can – just about – squeeze under. I add another, smaller, sheep hurdle. The following morning, she is standing on the field side of the fence to my lawn. She is staring at me. I am inside at the kitchen window. By the look on her face she is not best pleased! I know that sheep are pretty stupid (I used to keep them) but this one isn't! She's resentful!

Benson and Nell

December 2022

Nell: The two sisters were dropped off on Saturday and they stayed the night! I really like them because they sit or kneel on the floor and cuddle and stroke me for ages. I'd stay there forever if I could. They tickle my tummy and I look at them adoringly. We go for a short walk in the dark – one has a torch – and it is really cold. I don't mind the little walk because I'd already been out with Benson earlier.

In the morning, she takes me into the paddock for a short time and then we go back to the house. The girls are still there and she makes them delicious pancakes for breakfast. She never makes me pancakes although I have to admit to already having had my own breakfast when one girl drops a piece of pancake. I immediately eat it so that she doesn't get into trouble!

She has been watching football on the television. I've noticed a ball moving and flashes of people running but I don't take too much notice. What I do notice is that when the television is off there's an outline of another dog in there. It's shadowy and moves a bit when I go up close but there's no dog smell. Who is it?

Me: My daughter was off out on Saturday night for her work's Christmas 'do' so the girls came to stay the night. They are so loving towards Nell and enjoy making a fuss of her. They are calm with her – a good thing as she's inclined to forget about the 'no jumping up' rule when excited!

I take Nell into the paddock while the girls are still upstairs. It's just a short walk as, later, we'll go with Benson. Then I make breakfast for the girls and we make Christmas angels out of card. One wants me to help her with a knitting activity while the other is drawing. A very cosy domestic scene until my daughter arrives. She's had a good time and is keen to get the girls home, so she rushes around collecting their stuff. Nell gets excited with all this bluster and seems sad when they leave. We are going out with Benson later so that will make her happy.

I am ready to watch England in the football World Cup and have my chocolate ready! (This is now a tradition that I share with my friends — a small piece of chocolate for each England goal scored!). I would say it's one of my five-a -day since chocolate is made from a nut but, even I, realise that is a stretch too far! However, mine is always very dark chocolate and, therefore, good for me! Come on, England!

Nell sometimes watches television; she's been quite taken with 'Strictly' — is it the bright colours and movement? – and has, occasionally, watched football but the funniest thing is when she sees her reflection in the blank black screen!

Nell: When I want to stand still and sniff something really interesting, she gets a bit fed up if I'm more than a few seconds but if she wants to stand still I have to wait forever! She was looking at the sky. Is it going to rain? I'm used to her singing quietly – I think I know most of the words to 'Father and Son' by now – but this standing still is disconcerting.

For two days we've been down the drive and she's picked up leaves. I don't pick up leaves – I go sniffing and exploring and I know enough now not to venture onto the road even when the big gates are open. I think she's beginning to trust me but she calls me back occasionally and gives me a stroke. I think she's checking up on me!

She loves me! I know she loves me! She let me sleep in the kitchen! The doors were open so that I could go out through the boot room to the outside, if I needed, but I could go back into the *kitchen where I also have a bed! I think I've got her trained, eventually!!*

Me: We're still walking early in the morning. Today, I stand still and watch the sky. The starlings have woken up and are meeting in a mass – some from different areas – and begin to make their swooping displays before heading off together. There are a few 'rogues' – those who fly solo, in a different direction and some who circle the periphery of the mass, flitting in and out as they fancy. I think that it correlates with human society and then feel a bit stupid being all philosophical on my own on an empty country lane at the crack of dawn!

The weather is wonderful; cold (very), dry and with bright sunshine. I take Nell with me to sweep up leaves down the drive. I can let her be free as she is now at the tail end of her 'oestrus' time. She explores and I rake, then collect up leaves. I can only manage an hour at a time as my shoulder reacts badly to repetitive movement but it's a lovely time out together in the fresh air. If it's still dry, we can do more tomorrow. Let me explain; it's quite a long drive with trees and, thus, lots of fallen leaves!

Freezing cold weather has made me think about where Nell sleeps; the boot room is like an air trap between the outside and the inside. Last night, it was bitingly cold and I opened the kitchen door and left her the run of the downstairs except for the sitting room, crossed my fingers and hoped that all my woodwork etc would still be whole by the morning. It was! She seems to appreciate the trust!

Nell: <u>She tried to give me something disgusting to eat</u>! She said in that coaxing voice "Here, Nell. Eat these" and I did put them in my mouth but ugh! Ugh! Not for me! What is she trying to do to me?

What is wrong with humans? They are creeping along the sides of the lane, going so slowly. Not their usual march — so strange.

Me: The dog who will eat anything — anything! — has spat out the worming tablets! I was so sure that Miss Glutton would just swallow them like a child with

Smarties (other sweets are available) but no! It seemed as though they'd been despatched down the gullet and, when I turned round, two white tablets were laying, forsaken, on the floor!

There was freezing ice in patches along our walk. Sandra and I went along very slowly compared to our usual fast pace. I am always full of trepidation about ice having once broken my leg by sliding over and, I think, Sandra is also being careful today as her strong wellies have not prevented a slight slip!

Nell: **I have had the very, very best week! Ever**! It began with my bestie, Benson. She and I walked with Sandra and Benson in Sandra's fields in the morning. It (the field) was white with frost and the humans were coated, hatted and gloved. Benson and I had a lovely race, played and we even paddled a bit in the stream. Benson had a big drink. Then, Benson came back to my house with her and came in! He began to sniff all around and picked up all my toys to test out. I didn't mind, I was just so happy to have him in my home. Then, Sandra came with Benson's bed and food and she left him here. He's staying! She called it a 'sleepover'.

Me: It is really cold. Probably too cold for snow! Instead, every morning there's a heavy frost – all the outside taps are frozen and there are some icy patches.

Benson is coming to stay as Sandra and Nick are off to Manchester for a few days to see their daughter before Christmas. As well as Benson, I also have the added responsibility of the hen; putting out her food and opening up the run each morning plus closing up the door at night (she puts herself to bed!). I am going to have Nell on the lead for these jobs!

On the first morning that Benson arrives with his suitcase (only joking!), Nell is excited and pleased; he's not been in our house before. She is so good at sharing her toys and even her beds. (Told you she was a hussy!) Benson tries all the beds and Nell tries his.

Nell: Benson and I were both tired and slept in the kitchen. Benson doesn't have to go out in the night to pee like me. I don't think he'd fit through the dog flap as he's so tall but how does he manage it?

We go out every morning, after breakfast, and race around the fields and then we do the same each evening. Sometimes, we both have a snooze during the day and sometimes we play with the toys. She says Benson needs his sleep, so I try not to be too bothersome.

When Benson and I were at the top of his big field, there were two big animals there. Benson took no notice of them so I, too, pretended to be indifferent. They both ambled away without even acknowledging that a potential threat – me – was watching them. Rude! It was worth copying

Benson because she said, "Good dog, Nell!"

Me: They spend the night in the kitchen and are ready to go out in the morning. I am walking them twice a day in Sandra's fields so that we don't all slide over on the icy roads. I had to go back one night because I couldn't see if hen was in and had to get a torch!

I think the hen situation under control and was also pleased and surprised that Nell ignored the sheep in the fields when we came upon them one afternoon. Two of Sandra's ewes — she says that they're Nick's — are expecting lambs imminently and are housed in a stable. Fortunately, arrangements have been made for 'ewe watch' by other neighbours! Although I've kept sheep (who had lambs) it was some time ago now and I'm glad that the getting up in the night to check is not on my watch — especially as it is so cold!

Nell: So much more excitement! I told you it was a good week! Benson is still here but two visitors have arrived with all their luggage! These have been before and I greet them with enthusiasm and they bend down to stroke me, saying, "Wow! You've grown! Good girl". I love all that!

After our walk later in the day, she puts Benson's bed and food back in his house and then he goes in too! I don't make a fuss, or cry, because there are two people to pat and stroke me in my house!

Me: My brother and sister-in-law arrive with cases, presents and food! Both dogs are welcoming. My 'townie' relatives feel the cold so the central heating is on all day and all doors are closed which means that Nell cannot let herself out. Benson's people are due home later this evening and so I take his bed and food back after our late walk. I don't like to leave him alone but have already made arrangements with Sandra that, if they cannot get home due to weather conditions, they'll ring me. I think it's best that he is there to greet them.

Nell: All sorts are going on here! People are up steps and laughing, there are boxes on the floor and exclamations of 'Oh! That's lovely, let's use that!' Strange things are being placed around and then the boxes go back upstairs. I know there's an upstairs but she has always told me to 'stay', so I don't go up there as **– I am a good dog!!**

Me: My relatives want me to try to feel Christmassy and so, consequently, out come the decorations. I have made cardboard angels to hang from the beams in the sitting room, accompanied by snowflakes. Cards are strung up in the kitchen and lights on the beams. I buy a small tree, in a pot, much to the disgust of my children and grandchildren. "You've got the biggest house and have always had a big tree", they snap. My thinking is – I can plant it out or let it grow in the pot and I can handle it myself without struggling! The tree looks pretty although, I admit to myself, that some of the lovely decorations are too big for it! There is more room, with this tree, in the sitting room.

Nell: When the visitors go, we are just the two of us again. She goes shopping and does stuff with paper and scissors. She does some cooking – more than her usual 'throw it together' meals.

<u>I've had the best, the very best, day! Ever! Ever! Ever!</u> In the morning we had a little walk. When we got back, there were phone calls and more phone calls and she was putting things in bags and boxes! I think, is she going away – again?! Some of the things are mine so am I going somewhere?

A car arrives and inside is Sophie! We both get in – me, too! I am in the back with Sophie and I copy what she does – I lay down. It's further than I've been in a car but, when we stop, everyone gets out. I had to be helped into the car and now I'm afraid to get out. The humans – there are three of them – are putting on their wellies. I have my lead put on and then I get down out of the car. So many smells! My nose is down and I am sniffing, sniffing and standing still. It is not grass, nor earth and not a road. Apparently, it is sand. I am let off the lead and we walk (the humans) and run (Sophie and me) over a few stones, then onto the sand which goes for miles and miles! There are thousands of dogs and people. I am so excited that I stop and greet them all! Most are friendly – dogs and people – and having said hallo, I run back when I am called. I splash in water and open my mouth - it is not nice – salty – but I run through the water with Sophie. Sophie chases a ball which is thrown for her and I run for it too! Sh! I think I am faster than Sophie (!) and get to it first most of the time – so – Sophie stops halfway and then takes the ball back as if she retrieved it by herself!

I don't mind her taking the credit because I love running!

Back at the car, dried, off we all go and collect the little girls (the grandchildren) who climb in with all sorts of bags and coats etc.

We didn't go to my house! We went to Sophie's house and there were more people to make a fuss of me. The humans are busy with food but we, Sophie and I, are tired and we sit quietly.

After the humans have eaten, they sit around and play some sort of game. I am still so tired, I don't nod off, but I keep out of the way as much as I can on my best behaviour until – I am so embarrassed and ashamed – I need a pee and don't know where to go. I am desperate and start to squat. SWMBO rushes over and LOUDLY, so now everyone knows, tells me to go outside and shows me while the puddle is cleared up. After that, she takes me out several times and I always pee but I don't get a treat – just a 'good girl'.

I have been given some presents! Actually, everyone gets presents but I got a pink pig, a squeaky pineapple, a ball and treats! I told you it was the best day ever! Ever!

Back in the car again, we go home to my house – all of us – to sleep the night.

Me: My brother and sister-in-law go home for their own Christmas with their family and Nell and I are back to usual except that I am busy wrapping presents etc.

On Christmas morning, I take Nell for a walk as usual and set to finishing the cheesy leeks and fresh fruit salad, which are my allotted items to make for our Christmas lunch. There are phone calls from family to say 'Merry Christmas'. Nell was watching me intently as I packed boxes and bags to go with us to Bude –

where my daughter lives and where we'll be having Christmas Day.

My granddaughters are at their Nanny's with their father, opening their presents, when my daughter, her partner and Sophie arrive to collect us and take us straight to the beach. There are so many people – and dogs; there's a Christmas Day swim at the beach in Bude which has just ended and that's why there are crowds – participants and watchers. I wonder how Nell will be as we are so isolated from crowds where we live. I needn't have worried. Nell absolutely loves it; she paddles, she socialises (humans and dogs) and she runs. Boy, does she cover some sand! And, although she's always good at coming back when called, I am so delighted that she runs back, despite the distractions, when we call her. She never seems to stop and just walk; she's on the racing side of running the whole time!

We collect the grandchildren on the way back to my daughter's house for Christmas lunch and are joined by her partner's grandparents.

We all have presents to open and jobs to do for the meal. The dogs are quiet now and behaving really well until – puddle alert! It's Nell, of course, and she creeps along, belly to the floor in embarrassment, when I send her outside. Of course, it's my fault for not showing her where to go earlier. No one makes a fuss, thank goodness! She has been so well behaved that no one can be cross – plus – she gets to use the 'still a puppy' card!

We are sleeping at my house tonight and so, when Ash's grandparents go home, we all pile into the car to drive back to mine: 'Mine' is a Devonian term for 'my house' which I had never heard in this context until I moved to Devon!

Children safely and exhaustedly tucked up in bed, we three adults flop in the sitting room with the two dogs. Sophie sleeps on her blanket upstairs outside a bedroom door and Nell, bless her, is unconcerned that she is not also upstairs but on her bed in the kitchen. All the adults are shattered and have an early night! I can be excused as I am much older but those in their thirties? The youngsters these days have no staying power!

Nell: The next day I thought we'd be back to normal but no! More people arrive and there is more fun and games

– Sophie and I go outside early with SWMBO but we later play outside with a ball and all the girls – and get very muddy!

There are more presents. Benson bought me a fluffy bird – she says it's a goose – and I love it! I bought Benson a squeaky apple because he liked mine when he came to stay!

Me: Boxing Day brings my son, his partner and my other granddaughter over. They carry with them 'leftovers' from their Christmas Dinner (with eleven people) and it is added to what we salvaged from my daughter's house. I have rustled up some chicken, freshly roasted potatoes and oven roasted vegetables. We think we can't manage more but I have bought sticky toffee pudding and chocolate brownie pudding (I know I could have made them but . . .). With left over fresh fruit salad we all tuck in again!

There are more presents and the three girls love their time together. We play more games!

Nell: I have been in the car again! Not to the beach, unfortunately, but to see the nice vet lady — the place where I get tasty paste!

I was good in the waiting room and I went on something to weigh me. Then I went in to see the vet who looked at my head. Other people came and gave me a cuddle but also came in with something that made a noise and went on my head. I was afraid of the noise but tried to be brave. I had some of the paste and the vet stuck something into my head.

There were two big growly dogs in the waiting room when we came out. I was quiet — I didn't want to draw attention to myself! When we got home, I slept and slept until it was time to go out with Benson and Sandra. We seem to be able to walk with them every day. Hoorah!

Me: Nell has a small lump on her head, above the eye but beneath her ear. I thought, at first, that it was a tick but it certainly isn't. Everyone has looked at it and offered advice(!) and I've decided to get it checked out at the vet's.

Nell waits patiently and is weighed – 21.8 kilos – before we go into the consultation room.

The vet has to shave the area in order to get a good look and Nell is quite placid. This vet has one of Nell's sisters who now weighs 28 kilos! Am I not feeding enough? Does Nell have too much exercise? I know she was the smallest pup but I feel as though I haven't done my best for her to 'catch up'.

The vet takes samples which are to be sent off for analysis but she is almost certain that it is a histiocytoma. These are, apparently, fairly common in young dogs and disappear on their own! Who knew? Fingers crossed that this is what Nell has. She must have felt stressed since she slept from getting home until walk time with Benson and Sandra. We've walked together every day in the holidays.

Must look up my dog's insurance to see if I can claim.

Nell: I'm worried that there's either something wrong or unappealing about me; the little girls are here and they are not giving me the usual cuddles on the floor. Are they frightened of me? Do I smell? What is it?

The next morning (they stayed the night), they are back to cuddles and strokes. I really don't understand these humans at all! Talk about contrary!

Me: Two of my granddaughters stayed on New Year's Eve and we had one of our 'midnight but not midnight' feasts! They appear to be frightened of hurting Nell by stroking her or giving her cuddles. It's because of the shaved area. This reticence doesn't last overnight and on New Year's Day we are all back to normal, thank goodness! I have to make the obligatory pancakes – "It's a tradition at your house, Grandma" – and Nell is lucky enough to have the last one! This has never been known before! She is grateful!

Millie throwing a toy for Nell

January 2023

Nell: She says "Don't worry. It will go away on its own". What is she talking about?

Me: Hoorah! Nell's lump is a harmless histiocytoma and will disappear of its own accord, according to the vet's phone call to me with the results.

Nell: We're back to normal and my New Year's resolution is to be a very good dog – even better than before!.

I show her that I can be trusted, loved and - and given lots of those Christmas treats by going up to her and putting my head on her lap and leaning against her. I think she likes it!

Me: We are experiencing the most awful rainy weather. Devon's winter is often like this and it makes everything and everywhere muddy. Ugh! I have a silver lining; Nell has become so loving and appreciative of any show of affection by me; my little shadow who looks at me so endearingly. . .

Nell: Benson doesn't walk with me every day now that Sandra is back working. I find I'm sleeping more during the day. Is it boredom? I still play – alone and with SWMBO.

Me: Nell has been sleeping quite a lot during the day. Sometimes, she is totally sparko, breathing deeply, stretched out along the bed and floor or curled up tightly. I wish I could do the same – be so oblivious of all around and sleep!

Nell: Benson had a ball today when we walked. He put it down. I picked it up

and ran for him to chase me. He didn't!
I still kept it but the humans called me
over, removed it from me and threw it
so that we both chased it. Benson
often puts the ball down so I pick it up
quickly and keep it! That's the game,
Benson!

Me: Walking with Benson and Sandra today, Nell
decided to revert to 'taste anything I'm not allowed'
and ate a bit of horse manure from the road. I
shouted (of course!) and Benson dropped the ball for
her to pick up. I wondered whether it was so that she
had something in her mouth and, therefore, couldn't
get into any more trouble, thereby proving that
humans give dogs attributes they value themselves!

Nell: She keeps pushing that noisy
thing around and glances at me as if
I'm making her do it! She moans about
'hair'. I wonder if she's worried about
her hair? It looks okay to me. My hair
I'm rather proud of; it's black and

glossy, really smooth on my head and ears – perfect! Sometimes, she brushes my hair and some of it comes out on the brush but there's still plenty left! I feel sprightly after she's brushed me.

Me: Having vacuumed the floors, I found myself wiping up some water I'd spilled in the kitchen – only a few drops – but my cloth came up with quite a few dog hairs on it! Only two minutes after vacuuming! Unbelievable! I wished, not for the first time, that Mr Dyson (other designers are available) could invent an attachment that has a dog brush/comb on it so that I could vacuum hair straight into the cleaner. I'm thinking that, if I did it every day, eventually the floor would stay dog hair free! The attachment would have to silence the motor or I wouldn't be able to get it near Nell who is afraid of the cleaner. In the meantime, vacuuming is happening daily and so no electricity is saved!

Nell: I've met some dogs out walking recently who don't seem to like me! I am always friendly towards others and so don't understand this growling thing. I know not to go too near though – I don't want to be bitten! One of the dogs – the one who looks like me – is wearing a muzzle, you know, that 'thing' over her nose and mouth. I haven't had mine for ages – she gave up on it! She's older than me, this dog. Hasn't she learned? Actually, I haven't learned but have the excuse of youth!

Me: We've met some different people with dogs while out walking. This is odd in such a quiet, isolated area. Some of the dogs have warned Nell off and she's taken the hint! This is a shame as she is so friendly and no threat. One, the Labrador, is wearing a muzzle. The owner explains it is to stop her eating revolting rubbish! So, I'm not the only one and his dog is much older than Nell!

Nell: Yesterday, I hated going out to start off with. The rain was hard and had ice in it. She made us stand in a little stone house for a few minutes until, she said, it had eased. Eased! It was still pouring down although, admittedly, not so much.

There's standing water across the road and even along our drive. She gets a bit cross with me for pulling on the lead along the road but I want to hurry to wherever we are going and back again! After each outing, I need to be towelled down. She doesn't like me rubbing against her legs – she says it makes them wet. She's already soaked so what's the problem?

Me: The joy of walking in the wind and rain wears off after a while – a week, maybe? This must be week five or six with only a few days respite in between. I'm not talking about a little puff of wind and a dribble of rain. Oh, no! I'm talking wind speed of forty plus and torrents of rain. We don't walk in the fields since I'd be sinking into the ground at every step and Nell would be aquaplaning through mud. Along the lane, all the ditches have been full for weeks and, now, the road itself is flooded in places never known before. I wear my waterproof trousers over my other clothes and so am hot and uncomfortable before we even set off! Yuck!

Nell: I saw it! A smallish creature went right in front of us! It went into the hedge but I could smell it all along the verge. I was so excited I couldn't stay still. I wanted to run after it – or, indeed, run anywhere!

Everyone looks at my head. I don't know why since the hair is growing back and the lump is now flat, but white. Will it go away totally and be covered by hair? I like to look my best when the family take pictures of me!

Me: The snowdrops are appearing all along the lane, where I turn right. Even though the hedge trimming scalped along the bank, the snowdrops, those lovely small signs of spring, have, resiliently, sprouted back into beauty.

A rabbit ran right across the lane in front of us! That was it for Nell – all the walking on the lead training went out the window and she was pulling!

Nell: She really scared me! There I was fast asleep when she came downstairs and it was still dark. I wasn't expecting her! I raced round to greet her but I think she wasn't prepared and I made her jump! I ran outside to the boot room, thinking there was someone there and out of my mouth came <u>a very loud bark</u>! It scared me!

Our yard was white. It was not frost like yesterday. Yesterday our yard was dry. It is cold under my paws. Guess what? She opened the gate and took me into the field! I'm off! I'm running,

running! It feels glorious! In some places there is some mud but not too much. We go round two fields. I go absolutely mad with the delight of running. She is laughing at me but in a good way. I was still feeling lively when we got in and I played with my toys.

Me: I wanted to extend the heating this morning so, when I heard it start up, I went downstairs to alter the timer. It was still dark. I must have surprised Nell who nearly bumped into me and then ran outside barking loudly! Nell never barks! Well, I've only heard her bark on a few occasions – one was when a ball went under a chest and she couldn't reach it and the other was when she was growling and barking quietly in her sleep! I'm pleased that she was afraid enough to bark. I wonder if she thought someone was breaking in? Yesterday there was some ice in places but this morning we have a slight covering of snow and frost. I think the ground will be frozen enough to go in the fields (and I don't fancy slipping and sliding along the road). Nell is delightfully thrilled! She runs. Then, she really takes off!   She's through the second muddy gateway into the top field and streaking across it. She's a joy to watch. I am about to pick up a small branch that has fallen and put it in the hedge but Nell is there before me and she trots proudly with it in her mouth. When she's had enough of that, she has the 'zoomies'; racing in circles, up and down, round and round! The forecast is that rain will wash the snow away and it has gone with the sun by lunch time. I'm glad we made the most of it.

Nell: She's gone off again! **Again**! This time she's left her son, Ben, to look after me. At least, I think he's here to look after me but he spends a lot of time playing guitar! Oh, and putting logs on the fire, as it's been cold. He has taken me out – we even walked with Benson and Sandra – and given me lots of cuddles.

Me: I went off to visit my siblings and to attend a belated party for my younger brother. I left my son,

Ben, to house and dog sit. I feel slightly guilty about him taking a few days holiday from work but he assured me that he needed the break and had an assignment to plan and write. He's good with dogs but I hope he doesn't do to Nell what he did with my previous dog – namely – double feed!

Nell: She has done nothing but nag me for two days! What have I done wrong? Worse, she's put the hose on me twice; freezing water sprayed over my tummy, legs and bottom. Then I have to be rubbed dry with a towel but, before that, she shut my dog flap with me on the outside! She didn't tell me that I couldn't get in and I rushed at it, the first time, and hurt my head but the second time I went right through! She was cross with me – again! She put the dog flap back but each time I came back into the boot room, the 'thing' came with me! It's fixed now but I quite liked the hole in the wall!

Me: Naughty Nell! Two days of walking with Sandra and Benson and Nell decided to get really filthy and smelly on both days. Day one: Nell went into the very deep water in a gateway. The water has been there for weeks and is deep and muddy. A car was coming so I called Nell but she stayed in the water and sat down! (I have told her to sit when there's traffic and she decided to do it there!) When she came out, she was covered with smelly, slimy mud. At home, I hosed off the filth and shut her outside, closing the dog flap (so that she didn't shake inside) and she almost bounced off the closed door. I was only going inside for a towel. Day two: She – good girl! – did not go in the gateway BUT she did decide to run along a ditch with stagnant water in the bottom – a new ditch run for her and, hopefully, the last! The result was a very smelly dog, another hose episode and a second dog flap closure while I went in for a towel. However, Nell was desperate to get in and in she came wearing the dog flap which had parted ways with its fixings! I looked at it in despair – the screws were quite short and so would need replacing and some plaster had flaked off around the wood. I pushed it back for the evening but each time Nell came in so did the flap!

Going out was fine. I am ashamed to say that I played the 'weak female' and asked Nick, my neighbour, for help. It was refitted in five minutes!

February 2023

Nell: I want to give her the benefit of the doubt; she left the logs outside the back door in the wheelbarrow so that I could have my pick! It was thoughtful of her because I usually get my own sticks from the field and when I try to get them into the house she says "No" and takes them away. Well, actually, she throws them over the fence so that I can't get them. When I get a stick or suitable log, I strip the bark off with my teeth (I'm very proud of my strong teeth) and then break off pieces of the wood that is left. She says it's messy. This morning, I chose a lovely couple of crumbly pieces and separated the bark from the inner. There were quite a lot of wood splinters but – and I'm proud of this – I didn't take any into the house. Was she pleased about my thoughtfulness? Was she heck! She seemed surprised that I'd chewed them. She'd left them there for me, hadn't she? Otherwise, she'd have taken them in as she usually does. I never, never chew the wood that she puts in the baskets by the fire. I know that is for burning and, as I am an obedient dog, I don't touch it! But this wood was kindly left for me and so I took advantage of it. She moaned about having to clear up the splinters and huffed, ignoring me, in that way of hers. I'll never understand her. What's a dog to do?

Me: This morning, after putting out the recycling, walking Nell around the field and loading the wheelbarrow with an assortment of logs, I felt entitled to have my breakfast before fetching the logs in. I made the mistake of leaving the wheelbarrow by the back door in readiness for later. Breakfast over, I went to get the logs which included some smaller pieces to use as kindling. What met my eyes? The little devil dog Nell had taken some of the kindling wood from the barrow and chewed it up! There were wood splinters all over the concrete and I had to sweep them all up. She seemed surprised that I was cross! The only consolation was that the mess was outside!

I have to admit to smiling though (I was putting the logs in the basket) when I nagged Nell again by saying "Who chewed my kindling?" and Nell headed for that dog she sees in the television and turned to look at me as if to say 'It was her!'

Nell: At long last – a run in the fields with Benson! We went round two of our fields, chasing each other and arguing over sticks, running as fast as we could! Then, while the humans talked outside, we carried on playing! It was wonderful! I've missed Benson, although it's only been two weeks since we last saw each other.

Me: It only takes Sandra and I thirty or forty minutes to walk round two of my fields but we carried on talking and, when I got in, suddenly we'd been out for an hour and a half! Obviously, we'd plenty to say! Nell was so pleased to see Benson and they certainly made the most of not having been together for two weeks. Whilst overexcitedly playing, Nell emitted a bark!

Nell: SWMBO (she who must be obeyed) and I had already been round the fields in the early morning but Sophie came with her humans and we all went round the fields again! I loved it! I tried to get Sophie to play Benson's game with sticks but she was busy examining who/what had been in the fields before us. When she'd done that, we played chasing each other. We also played in the house but were told off a few times for racing round the kitchen! It was worth being told off!

We went onto the lawn for more playing and I have to admit to being tired when the visitors left!

Me: Half term brings my daughter and two granddaughters here plus Sophie, the dog. Valentine's Day today and, although only half-way through February, the day is glorious; dry and sunny. There is some warmth in the sun. We walk the fields and the dogs run and play. Sophie is interested in sniffing everything and everywhere. Nell keeps trying to get Sophie to play by enticing her with sticks. We are nearer home when Sophie agrees to play chase. They also played in the kitchen, covering the floor with lots of dog hair! When the girls think to go in the tree house (a hut on a tree stump), we are all outside in the sun again and there is more chasing. Nell will sleep well tonight!

Nell: I think I've worked out what that thing is that she watches. Sometimes there are bright colours on it and at other times it's blank. It only has pictures when she sits down in the evening. It must be something to entertain her but she controls it. I thought it my job to entertain so I always get out my toys, when we go in the sitting room, to get her attention. I have to admit though, that I too have watched it! There was a cat I saw and also some dogs. I would watch it all the time if they were always on!

Me: Nell has been watching television! She is very interested in the cat who is getting fed – an advertisement – but she's always aware when there are dogs on! However, she still looks at herself in the blank screen. Perhaps that shadow is an alter ego ('don't get carried away', I tell myself, that's a different story!) or, maybe, it's reassuring for her.

Nell: During the night I was very bored and my teeth are playing up so I went into the boot room and had a little nibble of the carpet. Well, it began as a little nibble but I got carried away and pulled up three corners folding them into the middle so that I could get to the rubber beneath. Then, finding I couldn't stop, I chewed off some of the carpet round the edges. It wasn't very nice but I couldn't help myself! **Boy! Was she cross**! She didn't know what I had done until we went into the boot room to get ready to go for a walk. I thought that we wouldn't go as a punishment. She kept telling me how naughty I was and it took her ages to put the carpet back under the big piece of furniture. I could pull the carpet up easily from under it. She's so weak! I must give her teeth strengthening lessons! Anyway, when we eventually got going I was really well behaved. I wasn't going to push my luck any further! I didn't want to upset her but I just couldn't help myself!

Me: I am ashamed at how cross I was with Nell: I blame myself but also I cannot help shouting at her. I should have nipped this behaviour in the bud long ago. When it was just the rubber edge of the utilitarian carpet being chewed away (not eaten, she's not that stupid), I felt that it didn't really matter but the rubber fetish has made a reappearance and this time it involves folding up three corners of the carpet that she can access and not only biting off the rubber beneath but also chewing off big lumps of the carpet itself. Moving the carpet means that she pulls it up from beneath a big settle that is heavy. On the morning I'm talking about, I had the devil's own job to get the remaining carpet back underneath; it involved lifting the settle and trying to get the carpet edges under at the same time. It takes both my hands to lift and I couldn't push the carpet back with my foot. I was so frustrated at my inability to put it back but I had to persevere or I couldn't open the back door! It wasn't helped since I was muscularly challenged by some unknown prior movement, making it painful. In the end, I angled the settle and managed to lift the end over the carpet. By this time, I was hot and bothered, outside it was dismal and rainy and Nell was quivering outside the dog flap after my angry remonstrations! There was only one consolation – sensing she'd better be on her best behaviour, she walked beautifully on the lead!

Nell: She seems to make lots of phone calls and does lots of reading. I am trying not to be too demanding and, at long last, I've got her attention in the evenings with my toys. I can catch some of the toys now, when she throws them, and she praises me! When I get fed up, I go off for a little snooze but then return before she's ready to go to bed. My thinking is, if I'm in evidence before she turns off the light, she won't forget my half bonio! She did buy me a bone and I am exercising my teeth on it. She always thinks of me when she goes shopping!

Me: I phoned the vet practice to get Nell booked in for spaying. I was sent a fact sheet explaining about laparoscopic spaying (keyhole, where only the ovaries are removed). This is an option. The other is complete removal of both ovaries and uterus – a more invasive procedure. I decided to go for the 'lapspay' as recovery is quicker and phoned for a date to book Nell in. Wow! Not this month! The earliest appointment was in March and on a date not preferred by me but I didn't want to wait until April as I fear that Nell might come into season again by that time. So, the date is fixed – I haven't told her!

Nell: Well! I don't know what got into me except that I hadn't seen Benson for a while.

I was constantly being told off! Goody two shoes Benson – who had, after all, taught me about water – was teasing me by going to the ditches and puddles but then coming away when called. I thought I'd show him how daring and clever I can be by going into a deep ditch filled with water. I took his ball with me. The ditch was really deep and I was a bit out of my depth but I wasn't going to show that so I kept going in and out even though I was being told to come out. I could see that she was cross that I didn't come out and stay out but by then I was having fun and afraid of being really told off!

I have to say now that I don't know why I went into the other ditch – the one nearer home. You know how it is – sometimes you just do something without even thinking? Anyway, in this ditch there was just sludge – a bright orange – and no water. I wanted to get out immediately but didn't want to lose face with Benson and I stayed still because a car was coming along. When I came out, I had this orange stuff glued to my lovely fur – ruining it. Benson seemed unimpressed by me so that action went down like a lead balloon!

At home, I got cold water hosed on me, then some warm soapy water and then more cold from the hose! The best bit was being dried with the towel and it made me feel clean and happy. I wanted to race around like a puppy. No! I'm not a puppy now - as I'm trying to prove to Benson.

The next day, she put me on the lead twice! Although she let me off again, I was humiliated. I think it was by the orange sludge and the deep ditch when I was on the lead but I'm not sure because I was too busy trying to walk nicely to take much notice. I didn't want to experience the 'cold shoulder' treatment of the evening before. I'm not too proud to grovel!

Me: I have taken a few days to think about writing the next part; I was feeling low – am I selfish having a dog on my own, especially a dog so happy with company? Have I failed in my training of Nell? Is she so bereft of attention that she has to demand it – in whatever way? Or – are these human characteristics that I am foisting on Nell?

This is what happened to elicit these thoughts: Nell was so excited to be walking with Benson (there'd been a break), who had a ball. They ran on as usual, chasing after the ball carrier. Near the half -way turn there is a deep ditch which was overflowing onto the road. Before the ditch, Nell had taken no notice of the deep puddle in the gateway (scene of a previous immersion) – good! Both Sandra and I had said "No!" when she neared it (it is very deep and I always think of the Vicar of Dibley sketch when we pass it!) but now she suddenly launched herself into the deep ditch! I think it surprised her that she couldn't touch the bottom and I believe she was swimming! We called her out and she's generally so good at coming when called. Not this time! Even though she was struggling, she went in and out of the water for the full length of the ditch. She had stirred up the silt at the bottom but was still fairly clean. She was very pleased with herself but also had that 'I'm full of mischief' look in her eye. We turned to retrace our steps and she was back in – despite being told not to – getting smelly water over her. We walked on and again she skirted the gateway puddle BUT, as we neared home some while later, she dived into a ditch notorious for its orange slime. She has never even looked at it before! She came out with orange stuck all over her bottom and legs. I was furious but also, embarrassed by her naughtiness, laughing a bit. I had to hose her, wash her with soapy water and then hose her again. When I was drying her with a towel, I felt sure she was actually enjoying the bath! Damn!

The following day, walking with our friends, I put Nell on the lead as we approached both areas of concern! She walked well despite Benson being off the lead! Sandra had dined out the evening before on the 'orange story'!

Nell: Sometimes, I watch that screen thing but last night I was hooked! I'm not sure what was happening but I had to keep watching a hand. It moved slowly and repetitively across a board thing. I was spellbound. I hope it's on again!

Me: Nell was totally absorbed in watching the television! She occasionally watches — some things just catch her eye — but this was different; she sat glued for at least ten minutes (I was on the phone) watching the late Bob Ross painting. The screen showed his hand mostly, collecting paint from his palette and applying it to his canvas. Was it his quiet, calm voice? Was it the hand close up; did she think it was going to stroke a dog? Was it the colours? I was fascinated just watching her!

Nell: She's taken away the boot room carpet! I know why but I still don't understand it. I only chew a little bit each evening. I chew it when she disappears up the stairs. I'm not sure what she does up there but she's gone for hours! I get bored and need to do something. She put, well, dragged the carpet outside into the cattle house and left it there! I could have played with that! Now there's just cold tiles and when I say cold, I mean really cold. Brrr! I am trying to make up for it by going over and putting my head on her knee. She doesn't totally ignore me but she's still cross! What will I do tonight? It isn't as if she didn't still feed me and give me a long walk this morning but she seems distant.

I went mad running in the field and admit I had a little snatch at something to eat. She said I should drop it and I did. I'd have thought that was enough to please her. What can I do?

Me: Do dogs have a second teething? Nell has surpassed herself in the boot room mat chewing category! Each evening, she nips at a bit more but, last night, she ripped up whole chunks and pulled it out from under the settle again. I was upset rather than furious; just when I thought she and I had settled into a suitable routine, bam! We're back to the start. I decided to roll up the carpet and take it away as it was ruined. This was easier said than done as it is (was!) quite big. I had to drag it out to the cattle house!

Nell went scatty in the field zooming everywhere including through some very wet and muddy areas as if she thought she might as well be hanged for a sheep as a lamb! With quarry tiles on the boot room floor both she and I have noticed how much colder it is in there – and draughty! I heard Noel Fitzpatrick say on the radio today (he was talking about the bond that exists between humans and animals) that If a puppy chews your slipper, you forgive it in thirty seconds but if your neighbour parks on your drive that ill will lasts for years! I felt he was talking to me! I do love Nell, and it is unconditional, but I feel a bit defeated today. I have to be totally honest – I don't know how to deal with it when I am disappointed with her behaviour – and mine! Oh, dear! I sound like the teacher I used to be . . .

Nell: We haven't seen Benson recently. She has muttered something about he's got visitors. Therefore, we walk on our own and I'm on the lead. I know I'm walking much better on the lead because she keeps telling me so! But then we met someone new. I was so excited to say hallo to this little dog – perhaps over-exuberantly at first, as it cowered behind its human. We have a few minutes greeting and then we're back walking.

Me: The sun was out on our walk and the wind cold on our faces but the snowdrops are still visible, although beginning to fade and the daffodils are bravely beginning to bud and some, even more bravely, flowering. I'll just say this quietly so as not to jinx it but I've spotted at least ten primrose flowers out – several in my drive! Soul lifting for me and Nell has sniffed them!

Nell: I just couldn't resist it! I've been so well behaved, especially when walking along the road but the smell was intoxicating and there it was, waiting to be snapped up! I give myself away to her (I'm not subversive) by going up to her wagging my tail. She knows and makes me open my mouth to 'leave'. The second lot of deliciousness I am more secretive about, but she still spots me. She's a detective! I leave it but, later, go back because I just can't resist. She's giving me the cold shoulder and no treat when we get in because, she said "You've had extra!"

Me: I hate cats! Well, that's not quite true – we had two some years ago and they were lovely in their way! What I hate is other people's cats. You know, the ones who like to deposit their waste in gardens other than their own. In this instance, it was mine. To be accurate, the offending and offensive items were in my bottom field and my drive. Nell was on them in a flash. Now she smells of cat excreta and I can't get the odour out of my nose! Ugh!

March 2023

Nell: She gave me a lovely treat! She muttered something about it being quite disgusting but natural! I don't care – it was lovely! Then, then! she was very, very cross about my redistribution of some bits of wire. I had pulled at them while she was away and one thing led to another and I was pulling big bits apart. It was a lot of fun! Being chastised was not a lot of fun though. It was good job I'd already eaten the treat!

Me: Noel Fitzpatrick is wrong! It is quite possible to be cross for longer than more than thirty seconds when one's dog has chewed through cables connecting the Sky aerial to the television, especially when one has bought a special treat for said dog from the pet shop and given it before noticing the ruined cables! (The cables run along the outside wall of the house.) I was so cross!

Running with the Pack   Day One

Nell: She told me that we'd be walking with the boys. I hadn't seen Benson lately as he'd had visitors but suddenly there were three dogs to play with, including Archie - who is my size. There was a ball - but Marley usually gets it and keeps it. I chased Archie and played puppy fighting. I got told off for this but Archie doesn't seem to mind. It was all good fun and I loved being with the gang. I had a 'leg hose' when we got back! <u>Worth it</u>!

Me: I was prepared! I'd left towels outside, expecting to be hosing and drying Nell after racing with 'the boys' -Benson, and Sandra's son's two dogs, Marley and Archie. Nell has a 'thing' for Archie(!) – they are now much of a size and seem drawn to play with each other. Unfortunately, Nell's play consists of trying to bite his back leg or tail! He's too much of a gentleman to growl or retaliate and we had to reprimand Nell until she calmed down. They were well behaved and not too muddy – Nell only needed her legs hosed!

Running with the Pack   Day Two

Nell: I was thrilled to see the boys again today. Marley had the ball again and I wasn't too bothered because I could chase Archie. I got told off again for play biting him but he, occasionally, tried to get me! He and I were playing by the deep puddle gateway and . . . forgot ourselves! In we went and I was winning and dunked Archie. We came out smelly and soaked. Neither she nor Sandra were pleased. The mud showed more on Archie as he's a fox red Labrador! On the way back, Benson, Archie and I played the carrying a stick game. Fun! Marley was only interested in the ball so we let him carry it!

Me: Of course, I'd forgotten to have the towels ready outside today! Nell, chasing Archie, caught up with him in the Vicar of Dibley gateway and pushed him under! They were both filthy and Nell needed the whole hose, soapy water, hose again treatment when we got home! She loves being with the gang and comes home tired. Hoorah! They are all funny together and show their personalities; Marley's god is the ball and it's all he's interested in, Archie runs and plays good naturedly with all (but can take the ball from Benson's mouth), Benson is like the elder statesman who, occasionally, deigns to join in the game but is, mostly, showing good behaviour and Nell, well, Nell is just madcap. I'm going to add 'at the moment' and hope that she is still developing!

Nell: **I don't know if I can ever trust her again**! She took me away in the car and into a strange place and left me there! Left me to the unknown! There were nice people, who made a fuss of me, but strangers! And then, and then! <u>they put me into a prison</u>! A prison, I tell you! Why? I have been trying to be so good and well behaved.

I'll begin with the morning: She got up very early (for her, though not for me) and gave me the smallest breakfast I've ever seen! I ate it. Well, so would you after a whole night with no food. Then, she took me for a little walk and it was almost still dark and then, when she'd had her usual breakfast (no half measures for her) she put me in the car and took me to prison.

Me: Nell can have a quarter of her normal breakfast before the spay operation (that I haven't told her about) if it is before six am. I struggle out of bed and feed her and take her for a walk before we leave. She's very good in the car. I've put her little teddy in my bag so that she has something familiar when she comes round from the anaesthetic. I thought that teddy was better than a bone!

We were early at the vet's – not our usual venue but the same practice – where some staff are already and are very friendly. Nell is weighed and checked and I sign the permission form.

Nell: In prison, they gave me an injection – but no tasty paste!

When I woke up, I was wearing a prison uniform – that's what it felt like! It was all over my body and my front legs! What is this place? I am still in the cage! There's a little dog next door who keeps on yapping and barking. I wonder what he's done to be put in here? I have a headache and so try to get attention by my talking strategy. (She calls it whining.) Huh! The people – they are quite nice – seem concerned that I am in distress. I AM! I've never been locked up before!

Me: I feel quite odd when I leave. I know it's better to just go – I always told parents that on a child's first day at school. "Don't make a fuss, that always makes it worse!" I've got a few tasks to do before going home – back to an empty house.

Nell will only be away for a day but it's quite weird to unpack the shopping and have a cup of tea without her beside me. I get a phone call before noon saying the operation went well but that Nell is making whimpering noises. I can hear her and there's another dog yapping. I forgot to tell the staff that Nell has never been in a crate. My fault!

Nell: Later, her daughter comes to see me. Obviously, I'm allowed visitors. Maybe it's for good behaviour. I am pleased to see her. She and a helper lift me into the back of her car and I have my teddy given back to me – and someone else's blanket! I whine all the time in the car. Where am I going now? The gallows?

I'm home! Her daughter took me (the little girls were in the car, too) home! I'm still in the strait jacket and she doesn't take it off. While I am on my bed, they all sit and eat their tea! Later, she gives me some food – but not much! It is, however, delicious. Chicken and rice -yum! I got a bit more at bedtime. Before bed she takes me for a short 'toilet walk' on the lead and she unpoppers the suit at the back – as if I'd make it wet!

I sleep well but I wake up early and whine. Is it all going to happen again? It can't have been a nightmare because I'm still wearing that 'thing'!

Me: Hannah, my daughter, who has an estate car – more comfortable for Nell – brings Nell home. Apparently, she whined all the way! She is nowhere near sleepy enough! Why? She's had an invasive operation and should be comatose. Neither is she refusing food! I've made the light meal suggested on the aftercare sheet and it's wolfed down!

The protective body suit that I opted for rather than the head cone/ring, is strange! I fold back the rear when I take Nell for a quick 'toilet walk' last thing. She is only to go out, on the lead, for necessary toilet walks and must be kept calm – no running or jumping for ten days. I hope she can manage that! If today is anything to go by, she'll be climbing the walls!

Nell cries at some point during the night but goes back to sleep and all is quiet. I wonder how she'll be tomorrow and – will she ever forgive me?

Nell: I get more of the delicious food the next morning and taken on the lead to go to the loo. Then I'm told to go on my bed! I do and then, later, I feel quite tired and spend the rest of the day on my bed asleep – when she's not taking me out on the lead to 'perform'. Back to normal food, very short walks on the lead but I can't do more because now I sleep and sleep . . .

Me: It takes Nell until the following afternoon before she gives in and sleeps and sleeps. Thank goodness. She needs the rest and calm in order to heal and recover. She doesn't seem to mind the body suit too much and has made no attempt to even sniff at her undercarriage! There's only one slight problem; she's obviously feeling a bit insecure and likes me to be near her. If I'm not, she cries. This means I have spent the last two days in the kitchen pottering or reading! Nell totally flakes out when I'm sitting reading. It's a good thing I have a weighty tome on the go!

Nell: She's put me in the car again! Am I going back to jail? We go somewhere I know; the tasty paste place and we sit in the waiting room. Then, we see the nurse who makes a big fuss of me – lovely – and looks at my tummy. She puts a thing on me which is attached to her! Weird! She gives me two treats and then I go home in the car. Back to snooze . .

She has given me a really big bar of something hard and tasty to chew. I like it.

Me: On the third day after Nell's op she has a check up to see if she is healing well. Her heart is listened to and her tummy checked. She has to continue with the body suit and have only short walks on the lead. I explain that she was quite lively after the operation until the following afternoon when she gave in to staying still. "Running on adrenaline" was the answer. She's not running on adrenaline now – her days are spent snoozing, short walks and proper sleeping! Hurrah!

Nell is still calm and I have bought her a solid block of yak milk, flavoured with mint.

Nell: Today, I was allowed freedom! The strait jacket was removed and I had a different dog bed. I felt quite refreshed and played with my toys. The suit went on at bedtime and I slept.

Me: One week on and I feel the need to wash the body suit! Nell smells doggy and it has got wet in the damp weather. While it is drying, I watch her but she has no interest in her clipped tum. What is funny is that, out of her suit, she takes her toys out of the box and has a little play but when the suit goes back on, she stays on her bed and the toys are ignored! Some 'learned behaviour' here!

Nell: Visitors this evening! Her son and his daughter came. I get lots of cuddles especially from Emily, his daughter. They stay for the night and I'm thrilled when more people arrive! I am feeling back to normal and play with everyone. Two of the little girls keep putting my toys along the floor and teasing me with them. There's a lot of singing in the house today! I like it! There's a lot of food, too, but not for me. Strange objects come in and go out of the kitchen. It looks as if a bomb has hit it!

Me: Mothering Sunday. My son and granddaughter arrived and stayed the night before. Nell was pleased to have different company! Today, my daughter, her partner and my other grandchildren arrive. It was lively; the eldest granddaughter had a karaoke machine for her birthday and the girls were busy practising for their 'show' while the adults, well, mainly the two men, were taking out the old fridge and replacing it with new – not so easy as it was integrated and they had trouble getting the unit door off the front! We have a 'picky' lunch – all sorts of goodies for everyone to choose from and I'm sure Nell found some crumbs! The two youngest girls try to teach Nell the names of her toys. She fails their tests! My son says to his daughter that although Nell is lovely she is also stupid. Emily takes umbrage at this and berates him about saying horrible things about Nell! He acknowledges reprimand and walks off but she retorts "I'm not done yet!" I love this 'protect Nell' from slurs thing although I'm not sure Nell has understood her brain power has been maligned!

Nell: In the car again! Where this time? It's the vet's again. While we are waiting, a lady comes in with a little puppy. I want to make friends but the puppy is on the lady's lap. I see the nurse. She gives me a lot of cuddles and I am submissive, showing my stomach to her and she feels all over it. The nurse and SWMBO talk a lot. I am very well behaved. I am allowed into the paddock, off the lead, this afternoon! Freedom!

Me: Last post-op check-up (ten days after said op). Nell is fine and the body suit can be abandoned totally! She is allowed to walk further and be off the lead in the paddock, gradually building up, during the week, to our normal length of exercise. The nurse and I discuss Nell's continued chewing and she explains that some of her second teeth are still moving, probably causing some irritation. (I think that the irritation is mine!) I ask if she will ever stop moulting. "No!" is the answer! Labradors are noted for their constant hair loss! We discuss the problem of weight gain after spaying; I can tell that Nell is fine on this score and can judge whether to feed less or more. The nurse says that Nell is still growing!

Nell: I seem to have a new lease of life! I'm awake early and playing with my toys making them squeak! I'm hoping it'll wake her up and she'll take me out early!

Me: Nell is behaving like a very lively puppy! All that pent up energy!

Nell: Two walks before half past ten! Hurrah!

Me: Where there were millions of snowdrops, there are now thousands of daffodils! I take Nell for a second walk of the day in order to drink them in before the predicted rain arrives! Oh! Primroses, too..

Nell: I, honestly, did not chew goose! I was tossing him in the air and catching him – that's how we play, goose and I, and his innards were falling out! I couldn't do anything about it. I just had to leave his 'bits' on the floor. She said, "What have you been doing?" She looked at all the toys and looked puzzled. Then, she examined my bed! She, eventually, put goose on the side!

Me: I thought Nell had been up to her 'decorating' tricks again! There were bits of fibre filling over the kitchen floor when I came downstairs. I looked at the four soft toys – no big holes! I looked at her bed – all zipped up and intact! I went back to the toys. It's goose! Goose has split his seam and not lost too much of his stuffing. My medical skills are, again, needed – suturing – let's hope I make a better job of it than I did of Nell's bed in the sitting room!

Nell: It's been such a long time since I was able to walk and run with my friend, Benson. This weekend, we went on both days!

On day one, Benson brought his ball along and we both had it in turns. She had told me, before we left, "No V.of D. puddles and no ditches!" I was so good but she still hosed down my legs when we got back because, she said, they were muddy!

On day two, we had Benson's ball again. I've learned to let go of the ball when I'm told 'leave' and so either Sandra or SWMBO took it, occasionally, and threw it for us to chase. Then, and I want to remind you I'm only eleven months old, I forgot myself and went into the V. of D. puddle. I was told "Out!" but I just stood still, unable to believe I'd crossed the naughty line, again! Then, so what?, I went through the ditch which was spilling out onto the lane and loved it! I came out all excited but coughing because I'd had my mouth open!

Near home, I heard a noise in the grass verge. I dug but missed it!

Me: Nell is so bouncing with pent up energy that I think two weeks post op she'll be fine with Benson. She has really missed him and they run together after a ball. Maybe, not as boisterously as usual (or as much as with the other boys) but still enough to make Nell sleep really well when we get home. By nine o'clock, she'd rallied and the toys were being played with!

Nell was awake early the next day; I heard her downstairs. She'd clearly fixed her clock change over while I was still sleepy! We were walking with Sandra and Benson in the morning, so she had to wait until nine thirty before going out.

Nell likes to climb onto banks and she keeps eyeing up the land on the other side of ditches and gateways – as though it's something that she hasn't discovered and must explore. We had to keep calling her down. All is fine, as yesterday, until she enters the V. of D. puddle and then, madness descends! Not satisfied with being soaked on her legs, she dashes all along the ditch which, after all the rain from last night, is full to overflowing! Sandra laughs, I am cross but I realise Nell just cannot help herself and she's so delighted with the feeling that I don't really begrudge her it.

At one point, Benson places the ball by her when she is considering another 'not allowed' ditch. What a sweetie he is to get her attention away from it!

Sandra noticed a small animal where Nell was digging the verge! Fortunately, Nell missed it!

Nell: I really, really don't know why I did it! If I had thought how upset she would be with me I certainly would not have done it! It's only, once I got started, I couldn't seem to stop. It was how disappointed she was with me that did it! She looked at the pieces, looked at me and I had gone outside to greet her but I went straight back in onto my bed and stayed there all afternoon. I didn't get up until she said she'd take me for a walk — even though it was raining again. Later, I put my head on her knee and did my best 'sorry' face. She gave me a little stroke. <u>I am truly sorry</u>. She hasn't cleared it up – she said it would remind me if she left it.

Me: I couldn't believe my eyes when I came back from shopping! The newish black rubber mat (outside for shoe wiping) was in pieces – many, many pieces. Nell was sitting on the back step looking guilty. What did she expect? Me to praise her? I said "Go in" and off she went – onto her bed and she didn't move until four o'clock. Four hours! I left the pieces because it was raining so hard and I didn't want to get soaked clearing up. I had bought a treat for Nell but she wasn't given it. Bad behaviour does not get rewarded. How long will this destructive chewing last?

Nell: We were up and out really early so I knew something was going on! Then, Sophie arrived – the family dog of her daughter. In she came with her bed, bowl and bag of food. The people didn't stop but Sophie did!

Later, her son arrived and spent most of the day with us. We, Sophie, Benson and Sandra went out for a walk. Sophie is slow! We had to keep waiting for her to catch up. Sophie, like me, also likes water! There was plenty of it and we were all soaked!

Me: Last night there was a storm which continues today – gusts of strong wind and torrential rain. Such a lovely day for my daughter's family to be driving to Norwich! While they're away, I'm looking after their dog, Sophie. I take both dogs in the little field but it is awash with sitting puddles and mud so I then take them into the paddock where the grass is longer and the water drains faster on the slope. I have to towel dry both dogs! Then, Ben, my son, arrives for a visit. We cannot go outside without being drenched so we talk most of the day! Mother/son bonding time!

Sophie, Nell and I meet up with Benson and Sandra at the end of her working day to walk – despite the rain. Halfway along our walk we decide that we couldn't possibly get any wetter but we were wrong! The rain becomes even heavier! It takes some time to dry the dogs before I peel off my soaked jeans!

Archie, Marley, Benson and Nell in the field.

April 2023

Nell: It is possible for Sophie to go through the dog flap (she has done it) but she doesn't choose to do it, so we have to keep opening the doors to see if she wants to go out. She also won't pee on the concrete in the enclosed area and has to be given the opportunity to go further out! I like it because I get to go too! It means that we go out about three times a day into the paddock and once along the lane with Sandra and Benson. We go out late at night too, in the dark! Exciting! Will Sophie stay forever?

Me: Sophie sleeps upstairs in her own house but I left her in the kitchen with Nell. She wasn't there for long last night! I was reading in bed when I heard the thump of her body settling itself against my door!

Fortunately, she wasn't too fidgety as I would have been awake all night otherwise, being a light sleeper! We walked down the lane in the morning but it was difficult with both dogs on leads, both pulling in different directions, so we returned to the paddock, there again at lunch time, out with Sandra and Benson later, back to the paddock at ten o'clock! I'll be worn out!

Nell: She gave Sophie and me a chew each – those that last a long time. We loved them! Sophie and I have 'play time' but we get told off for chasing in the house. We play in the paddock and out in the yard. Sophie doesn't always want to play – she sleeps more than me.

Me: The vacuum cleaner had to work overtime today (and probably every day that Sophie is here) collecting up enough dog hair to make a small jumper! Why aren't both dogs bald?

Nell: Where does Sophie go at night? I sleep in the kitchen. Sometimes I sleep all night on my bed but, if I am awake, I play with my toys. Sophie came downstairs with SWMBO today. Why? She's my person, SWMBO, and I'm good at sharing but there's a limit!

We walked again with Benson. He and I were racing everywhere – although not as much as we usually do – and Sophie was busy peeing everywhere and sniffing all along the verges. She doesn't play with the sticks like we do. Benson and I played the 'share the stick' game as we ran along but our sticks seemed to frequently break!

Sophie likes to sleep in my bed in the sitting room when we go in there in the evenings. I don't mind. I went into the kitchen for a bit. When Sophie wants to play with me, she rolls onto her back, offering her tummy. I'm a dog! I don't do tummy rubs! I like them done to me!

Me: Coming out of the bathroom last night, used as I am to be crossing the upstairs hall to my bedroom in the semi-dark, I almost went flying over the recumbent form of Sophie – right outside the bathroom door! She was upstairs early! Maybe, tired out after the two days of running with Benson and Nell had exhausted her! I say running but that is a slight exaggeration – fast walking is better!

Both dogs were sleepy today, Sophie more so than Nell. It was dry – hoorah! – but when we walked with Sandra and Benson, there was water still in the ditches (full) and the V. of D. gateway. Today, it was Sophie's turn to try them out! I don't think she could understand why we were calling her out! We have a new mantra, Sandra and I, and it goes "Come on, Sophie!" as she is always lagging behind! I don't think she was 'team leader' once and was usually behind the humans. She is also the only dog I've met who seeks out, and eats, goose grass!

Nell: I can outrun Sophie! In the paddock, I made her chase me for a stick and I ran rings around her! Ha! We had a great game and then Sophie joined in the two of us carrying the stick game but she got fed up quickly and settled down to take the bark off the stick. While she was chewing, I sneaked in to steal! Clever me! I ought to be careful because when we are play fighting and she gets fed up with me she can be scarily fierce! I need to watch it.

SWMBO put Sophie behind the gate when she was weeding. Why? I was allowed out and, though I say it myself, behaved as well as I possibly could. If I went too far away, exploring, she called me back and I sat by her. I was told "Good girl" and got cuddles! Maybe this is what I should be doing all the time. It feels good.

Sophie's people picked her up this afternoon. Now I am alone again – well, obviously SWMBO is here – but no dog friend. Actually, I'm quite tired so I don't mind!

Me: Sophie's last day and it is lovely and sunny. I decide to do some weeding and clearing outside. Nell is being very well behaved and stays close to me but Sophie finds the small stream (with the 'trip trap' bridge) in front of the paddock and, before I know it, is soaking wet. Anxious not to let Nell see – she has never noticed this stream – I put Sophie 'behind bars' to dry off. I weed the other side of the tall gate, where she can still see me. All the dog towels are on the washing line and it takes some time for her to dry 'au naturel'!

Nell becomes a little sneaky when she and Sophie are playing in the paddock. She waited until Sophie was shredding a rotten stick then crept up and pinched the bigger piece! At lunchtime, I gave each of them half a bonio and Sophie's broke. Nell had whipped a piece away before Sophie knew anything about it. This behaviour will get her into trouble if she's not careful since Sophie is much heavier and with bigger teeth!

Nell slept and slept when Sophie left! She must have been very tired– she didn't even come into the sitting room in the evening except to check that I was there and then return to her kitchen bed!

I had hoped that Sophie would teach Nell to bark when anyone or anything comes into our yard. Those hopes are dashed, although Sophie did bark when there was a delivery (not for me as it turned out – but at least she'd alerted me in time to catch the driver) and Nell's reaction was to race out through the dog flaps to greet whoever was there!

Nell: Only two days later and Sophie's girls – the granddaughters – arrive here early in the morning. They always make a big fuss of me – which I love! They stroke me, give me tummy rubs and lots of cuddles. And the best bit is that they stay the night. They go to bed early and that's when I have a well-earned sleep – entertaining is quite tiring! There's another advantage to them being here; sometimes crumbs of food are inadvertently dropped and, always willing to help clear up, I snaffle them! SWMBO weeds outside while the girls play on their scooters up and down the drive and yard. I am outside all the time and it is such fun! At one point, she and I bump heads. She makes such a fuss! I didn't but then I'm brave and strong!

I am sorry when the girls go home but they say "See you soon!" as they leave and I think that means they'll be back shortly.

Me: I am looking after my two granddaughters for two days as it's the Easter holidays and my daughter was unable to book her holiday at the same time. We play board games when it is raining and go outside when it isn't! We are in and out, with Nell, on both days. Nell loves it; she gets so much attention and exercise. As I am weeding, kneeling and bending forward to pull up a big piece of root, Nell hurtles towards me and dips her head to lift it just as she arrives. There is a bone crunching clonk. Nell continues on her way but I have to ask Millie if I am bleeding as my nose and eye socket hurt so much. I am not bleeding but there'll be a bruise, if not a black eye!

I am asked to set Harry Potter questions for the girls to answer but they know more than me! (I read all the books as they were published but that was quite a long time ago!) I teach the girls to play 'Cluedo' – adult version. I don't know about Nell but I'm tired when they go home!

Nell: We were outside – I was exploring and SWMBO was on her knees pulling up greenery – when Benson arrived! He and I played for a long time until Sandra called him back. We'd had such a good time. A day or two later, when she was still on her knees, I took myself down the lane and found that I could get into Benson's place through the hedge. He wasn't there – out the front – so I wandered around but not for long because she called me back and told me off for going to his house! Why? He came to mine and that was acceptable. One rule for one and a different one for another! **So unfair**!

Me: Sandra has visitors for the Easter weekend and so Nell and I walk alone. The weather is kind – sunny and windy – and I try to catch up on the weeding (of which there is much) with Nell outside with me. Benson took it upon himself to visit one afternoon; he just arrived and began to play with Nell! I rang Sandra to enquire if he was 'allowed' and she said that he could stay. She came to collect him after some time. They'd had such a good play. However, Nell decided to reciprocate the visit a day or two later and took herself to the front of Sandra's house while I was gardening. I looked up and spotted her in the front garden. Fortunately, she came back immediately and I told her "No! Not our land!" She was bewildered. Sandra and Nick have a big pond – with fish, in the front – and, at the back, the one chicken and sheep. I couldn't trust Nell with those enticements!

Nell: We had such a great day!! All the little granddaughters came with their adults and Sophie! I was so excited! I knew something was up before they arrived as SWMBO was preparing food and there were so many delicious smells! All the humans were happy and chatty and Sophie and I played chase inside! Actually, we were kept inside, Sophie and I, when most of the others were having a good time (by the sound of it) outside. It was made bearable by the fact that it was Sophie, as well as me, who was not allowed out. All their fun seemed to go on for a long time but, eventually, we went out and had a lovely race game.

The humans ate and then we went outside for a proper walk in the field. I love it when everyone is there; I can run backwards and forwards to each person or group. It was interesting when the humans played games – they were running/walking and dropping strange things. I was told not to touch those strange things but, in the spirit of helpfulness, I picked up one of the wellies being used as some kind of marker and carried it around so I could join in!

It was quiet when they all went home but I was quite tired. I'd had a lovely day – games, running and so many cuddles! Perfect!

Me: Easter Monday saw my family descending on Nell and I for the day. We had our traditional egg hunt for the children but, this year, I asked the other adults to hide the eggs (not only eggs but chocolate rabbits, hair slides, decorative chicks!) while I cooked us all a roast. Then my granddaughters hid an Easter treat for each adult – having spent some time deciding where; there's a lot of hiding places outside! I kept both dogs with me (no chocolate for them - too dangerous for dogs) but when hunting outside was over there was a race and playtime for them.

After our (very filling) lunch, there were egg and spoon races – with some very bad cheating from the adults – and a strange new tradition where a rather large and elaborate, some might call it tacky and hideous, cloisonne egg is hidden by me and kept for a year by the finder! Did I not tell you we are a strange family? A cup of tea, a game of Cluedo and then Nell and I sat, both exhausted, until I noticed just how much hair both dogs had moulted over my house and out came the vacuum cleaner – again!

NB. Sophie disgraced herself the following day in her own house by eating the contents of one girl's egg basket – left on the kitchen table. She had to have an injection at the vet's to induce vomiting. Perhaps I am lucky that Nell only sneaks sticks and wellies to chew!

Nell: I've been noticing something in the trees by the river at the bottom of the field. The something is high up and moves quickly. What is it?

Me: Nell has barked! Twice! Both times at a squirrel she can hear, and occasionally see, in the trees at the bottom of the field. The river is fenced off but Nell runs up and down excitedly thinking she can catch the squirrel!

Nell: Just when we are settling back into our routine, SWMBO and I, we get Millie for a day. Millie is the youngest granddaughter and I know that sometimes she is a little scared of me. I think it's because I get so excited and I run around her. We have a lovely day although the weather isn't great it doesn't rain all the time. We go for a walk and they throw things into the water. Why? When we come back, we go into the paddock and they spend some time at the 'goose house'. I'm really nosey about what they are doing. Later, we go back to the goose house and some papers are suspended from the beams. It's all mysterious but they're having a good time and so am

I because we're all outside! When Millie's mum comes to collect her, we all go to the goose house again amid much laughter!

Me: Only one granddaughter today and I'm worried that she might find me the 'last resort' for her as her sister is off adventuring on a climbing treat. However, we share pancakes for breakfast (of course) and take Nell out. We play Pooh sticks but not with sticks! Sticks have been getting caught under the bridge where we play and so we use bits of greenery instead! In the paddock, Millie goes into the goose house, (which once was home to some geese) which has a half door. I decide to ask if she serves tea to passing walkers and water to dogs. Millie is off and running with this role play opportunity and the rest of the day is spent making signs for what is to become the 'dog friendly café' – all food items homemade! My task is to help in affixing these signs which must be inside (so as not to get wet or blown away) but also visible from outside for the customers to see! Nell has a whale of a time as we are backwards and forwards from the house to the paddock. The Dog Friendly Café is 'opened' by her mum when she arrives. She has to do the honours making a short speech and cutting the ribbon while wearing a hat! One of the reasons why I haven't moved house is because of this opportunity for outside play/adventure that this property provides.

Nell: I am one! Today is my birthday! A whole year ago I was just a new-born puppy – the smallest of the litter, I'm told. Now, I'm big! I have my own home! I have fields and lanes to run in! I have SWMBO! Hurrah!

Me: Nell's birthday. I have bought her a 'retrieving' toy and given her a special chew. She's been with me for ten months; some of the time has dragged and some flown but I can remember her as the tiny pup I first saw! Aah!

Nell: I had a great time today; a walk with Benson and Sandra was enjoyable even if I had to have a leg hose when we got home. Then we had visitors for the evening – her friends. I made a big fuss of them and they of me. I think I was able to entertain them all evening – I did my best.

Me: Nell and I walked with Sandra and Benson – we hadn't seen them for two weeks. Nell, of course, went in a ditch. She decided that she didn't want a leg hose when we returned and nearly pulled me over when I started the hose! She redeemed herself by being really sociable (and lovable) when my friends came to dinner!

Nell: I really don't know what was happening to me! I felt really scatty but also irritable when we went out with Benson and Sandra. Why? I saw something in the little copse along the lane and I was off, like a mad thing! I came back when called but there was something in there that had excited me and I didn't forget and, on the way back, I went in there again! And . . . I went in the deep puddle! When she called "Out!", I just stood there. She was not amused. Nor was Sandra this time. Benson had his nose in the air as if he didn't want to be with me, his friend! She put me on the lead! On the lead while Benson was free! How embarrassing! She didn't let me off until we got to the end of the lane, turned around and passed the puddle again! Sometimes, I don't even like her! When we reached home, she put my lead on so I knew I was in for a hose wash and I was feeling 'bitey' so I bit the wire on the wall! (She had gone inside for a few minutes and didn't notice.) She gave me the cold hose again! I sulked when she told me off about the wire which she discovered when she tried to switch on the television. She took me outside, showed me the wire and I crept on my belly to her but she was having none of it and just said "On your bed!" We both stayed in the kitchen for the evening. I don't know why I do these things that annoy her!

Me: It wasn't as if Nell hadn't had any exercise when we went out with Sandra and Benson; she'd been out first thing in the morning and again at lunchtime. They were both short outings, I'll grant you, but walks none-the-less. However, she was maniacal when we set off with our friends; firstly, she raced into a neighbour's small copse – which she'd never attempted to go in before. Secondly, she went in the Vicar of Dibley puddle and just stood, defiantly, in it! I put her on the lead and kept her on it until we 'd passed it on the return journey. The problem is that I'm not sure she associates the hosing (necessary) she receives when we get home with the immersion in puddle or ditch as it's a minimum of fifteen minutes later. Was I wrong to put her on the lead? Will she associate being on the lead with being told off? She returned to race, scattily, in the copse on the way back past. Why? I needed to go to the loo so left Nell outside before I got out the hose. I assume this is when she chewed the satellite cable – again! Was this spite? She realised she was going to be washed and didn't want it – although she really likes being dried with a towel! (I only found out about the cable when I wanted to watch something on the television in the sitting room.) I found myself saying to her, angrily, "You like water!" while she was hosed! So childish! I don't wish to put human emotional development stages onto a dog but it was just as if Nell was being a truly stroppy teenager. I wish no disrespect to teenagers. I can even remember the need to be rebellious myself!

An aside: I think I've worked it out! The reason that Labradors have a reputation, often proved in fact, for being fat and slow is because, when they're young and constantly chewing and destroying their owner's belongings, they are given lots of food – hidden in Kongs, given as treats, making them feel full and comatose and without the inclination or energy to chew anymore! The food intake becomes, then, the norm, a habit, even when the puppy chewing has stopped! I'm not joining the 'stuff 'em full so they don't move' gang but, when looking at my ruined mat and wiring, and having put forward this premise, I'm tempted!

Nell: SWMBO is quite odd! Have I told you this before? She had a conversion with a bird in a tree the other morning and she is always looking at flowers! I told you – odd!

Me: I am thrilled and delighted! There are violets growing at the edges of the big field with the primroses. Also, there are primroses, violets, and now, bluebells in the paddock! Not a little win but a big win! They're something to lift the gloom of a dismal day.

 Who would believe that despite the ditches being full, rain frequent and often heavy, we have a hose pipe ban coming into effect? Nell will be pleased!

Nell: I really like snuggling up to SWMBO! She usually strokes my head and ears – she's very fond of my ears. I heard the family say that I've grown into my ears but not my tongue! What did they mean? (I might have been panting as we were in the field at the time.)

I love being outside and hope that it is dry every day so that we can be out working. I say working — she does digging things and I collect bits of wood to chew and play with. She throws the ball thing for me and I, to please her, chase it for a while but I really like to spend time doing my own thing!

Me: Nell has (almost) stopped using peoples' legs as brakes when she runs to greet them. Not a bad thing as she is getting heavier. I noticed this when I was weeding; she comes beside me and leans in. If I raise my arm to pull out a weed, she insinuates her head, then her body, beneath it to get even closer. It's actually rather lovely but she is also inclined to sit or lay where I am working!

I have sprayed the newly fixed cable with 'no chew' spray. Fingers crossed.

Nell: I'm beginning to suss out all the different places in the field where I can identify who or what has been there. I spend a lot of time sniffing! But now the birds are nesting above the back door again and are swooping over the grass in the fields, they have to be chased! I don't really expect to catch them but I adore the running!

Me: When Nell smells or hears something of interest, she stands, tail straight out behind her, one front paw raised and, for once, is still. I think it's sometimes moles that she can hear under the ground. There are many mole hills in the fields! Fascinating!

Nell: I don't know what makes me feel so 'bitey'. I'm not sure if it's my teeth playing up or just an itchy feeling that only biting seems to assuage. I took myself outside quietly. I must have known that I was going to do a naughty thing as I didn't want her to know I was going out! (If I race out, as I usually do, the dog flap closes quite loudly after I've gone through. If I go through it slowly and carefully, it doesn't bang.) There was nothing outside to calm the instinct so I examined the wiring and found a little loose bit as it went round the corner. I'd just started to see if it would pull away and – there she was! **Caught!** I abased myself and then ran in! She's put some chairs in the way now!

Me: I caught her at it! Somehow, I just knew she was up to no good and I went outside. She looked so guilty! She crept past me and then raced onto her bed in the kitchen! I examined the wiring; at the corner, there was a small gap between wire and wall and I could see there was a slight dent in the wire. The wire there is painted the same colour as the wall and some of the paint was off – not much – as yet! (Is she trying to stop me from watching television in the sitting room?) I carried over two more garden chairs from their storage place and placed them in front to make the wire inaccessible. I had sprayed all the wire with 'no chew' but I did it all again just to be certain! Now the outside wall is arrayed with chairs like a waiting room!

Nell: I am a failure as a tracker! Well, not a tracker but as a 'spotter'. I pretended that I'd known all along that there'd been a deer eating in the field and that I just wanted to sniff where it'd been! No harm in a bit of bravado acting; 'a deer, who cares? Two a penny!'

Me: I looked again and there, some distance away, happily munching grass was a brown shape. I knew it was a deer. Nell was sniffing out something in a patch of tall grass, totally oblivious. The deer raised its head, noticing us for the first time. I carried on walking, wondering how long it would be before Nell saw. The deer had gone, elegantly leaping the fence before Nell caught the scent and pretended not to be too bothered!

Nell: She gave me one of my new toys and I played with it outside. She threw it – it goes a long way, - and I fetched it and raced around carrying it, doing the 'zoomies'. Such fun! It tires me out!

Me: I think I've got something sorted; wearing out Nell means a quiet time indoors and no chewing! A field walk in the morning, lots of throwing of toys outside and more walking later. It's working! And – Nell is now very good at 'leave', giving up the toy to be thrown again! Please don't let it rain too much as rain stops outside play!

Nell: I've decided that I've told you pretty much all about my life (so far) here in Devon. I hope I have many more adventures but you'll have to imagine these yourselves! (Note the plural – yourselves- since I hope that more than one person reads this.) For me, there's running, socialising, eating, cuddles, playing and more fun to be had. For SWMBO there'll be more nagging – of me! – and walking - of me! -and feeding – of me! She's not a bad old stick. I think I'll keep her!

Me: Nell and I have decided to close the diary as she is now one (and considers herself grown up!). She is such a sweet dog really, despite the chewing and eating of disgusting things – actually, this has all pretty much stopped. She has begun to sit by the fence adjoining a neighbour's field and waits patiently for the two horses to come over and greet her! She feels that everyone, humans and animals alike, must all be her friends as she wishes to be theirs. This is such a lovely outlook – I think I'll keep her!

Benson

Nell with goose.

Post Script July 2023

Nell has just had her annual vaccination and was described by the vet as a 'happy and healthy' dog. Much as I admire those owners whose dogs are completely well trained, I also like a bit of character to show. Nell is not the 'best ever' trained dog, but she does come when called and now she (usually) sits to order, 'stays' when told and (sometimes) walks well on the lead. She 'leaves' objects when told and plays alone or with me, bringing me her toys. She is a constant source of laughter for Sandra and me when she pounces on thin air in the fields, jumps, turning in the air to try and catch moths or butterflies or thinks she can catch the swallows swooping across the tops of the grasses. She likes to 'grass surf,' making herself wet – such a water baby. Above all, I loved the vet's description of 'happy'. Who could ask for more?

Acknowledgements

Nell: My thanks go to my breeder, Mell Lowe, for the first eight weeks, my vets, Penbode, for the cuddles and tasty paste, to my neighbours and friends, Sandra and Benson, for putting up with me. My thanks too, to SWMBO, who helped me to physically write my diary (no hands, only paws!). I have allowed her some creative licence with her recounting- in the interest of balance. However, much of what she has written is emotive rather than factual!

Me: And, after that, anyone else who knows me!

Thank you, Val Green, for computer wizardry with page set up, your patience with me changing my mind and the laughter!

I would like to acknowledge Simon Goodman for giving me (unbeknownst to him) my 'writing voice' – an ability to find humour in odd situations. Thank you, Simon.

Contact Nell on: nellandswmbo@outlook.com